Rod and Staff's Fifth Reader

I know that, whatsoever God doeth, it shall be for ever: nothing can be put to it, nor any thing taken from it: and God doeth it, that men should fear before him.

FROM ECCLESIASTES CHAPTER THREE

A TIME TO
PLANT

EDITED BY MERVIN J. BAER, R.S. LeBLANC,
AND MARVIN EICHER

ILLUSTRATED BY RUTH HOBBS AND LESTER MILLER

Rod and Staff Publishers, Inc.
P.O. Box 3, Hwy. 172
Crockett, Kentucky 41413
Telephone (606) 522-4348

Copyright, 1982
Revised, 1991, 2005
by
Rod and Staff Publishers, Inc.
Crockett, Kentucky 41413

Printed in U.S.A.

ISBN 0-7399-0405-1
Catalog no. 11501

2   3   4   5   6   —   16   15   14   13   12   11   10   09   08   07

Introduction

Many years ago the apostle Paul wrote to Timothy, "Give attendance to reading." He wanted Timothy to read the Scriptures with care and understanding. We likewise should "give attendance to reading." In this reading course, you will learn more about reading as well as listening, speaking, and writing.

As you examine *A Time to Plant,* you will discover that every twelfth lesson is a composition assignment. Does it seem strange to have composition in reading class? One of the reasons for reading is to learn to write. Writing is an important way of sharing our thoughts with others.

This reader also includes poetry. As you look at the table of contents, you will notice a number of titles printed in italics, *like this*. These are the titles of the poems in this reader. Every third selection is a poem or a composition assignment. Three of the poetry selections are Bible poetry from Psalms and Isaiah.

Short stories are a favorite kind of reading. Over half of the stories in this reader are of boys and girls about your own age. You will read about things that happened several hundred years ago, which will give you a picture of life and customs in former days. You will visit faraway places such as Scotland, the Philippines, and the Arctic. You will also read about the life and habits of animals such as beavers and teals, about traveling down the Mississippi River on a raft, and about the excitement of rescuing two little boys on a cake of ice.

Use your dictionary often. It is not enough to be able to pronounce every word or to read with great speed. It is more important that you understand what you read so you can learn the lessons of honesty, courage, and kindness that the stories teach.

The selections for this reader have been chosen carefully to provide you with wholesome, worthwhile reading. Though you will enjoy this reader, keep in mind that it should be more than just an interesting book to read. May you apply yourself to the helps that are given. As you develop your reading skills, it will benefit you in your other school lessons and help to increase your appreciation for God's "reading book," the Bible.

CONTENTS

To Market

AUTHOR UNKNOWN

Nenet and Manuel had been to market many times with Mother. When she needed only one or two things, they went alone to the little grocery store at the corner of their block in the wide and beautiful city of Manila in the Philippines. But they had never gone alone to the big covered market where people came every day to spread their wares on tables or in booths or on the ground.

"I am very busy today," Mother said. "I have no time to go to market."

"Manuel and I can go to Pedring's store for you," offered Nenet.

"But I have a long list to buy," said Mother. "Pedring's prices are higher than prices in the Quiapo market."

"We can go to Quiapo[1] for you." Manuel stood tall to show that he really was big enough to go alone with Nenet.

Mother looked at her children steadily. She thought of the ride by bus or "jeepney," of the many

[1]Quiapo (kē ä´ pō)

9

winding streets that looked alike, of the crowds in the big, covered marketplace. Then she saw how tall they both stood, waiting for her answer.

"I'm sure you can go alone," she said. Then she handed each of them a big marketing bag woven of buri palm. To Manuel she gave six pesos to carry in his safest pocket. To Nenet she gave the list of groceries.

"If you shop carefully, there will be some money left," she said. "You have not had a treat for a long time. Save twenty centavos for your jeepney fare home. Then you may spend what is left for sweets or toys."

Manuel and Nenet were discussing how they would spend the extra money while they stood at the corner by Pedring's store, waiting for a bus marked "Quiapo." They stopped long enough in their talk of candy, yo-yos, balls, and dolls to wave their hands at a thin little girl who was looking out the upstairs window over the grocery store.

"Poor Angie," said Nenet to Manuel. "She has been sick for weeks. She never gets outdoors to play. She hasn't anyone to play with her."

"She never has fun like we do," agreed Manuel, "going to market and everything."

Just then they saw the jeepney labeled "Quiapo." They were glad it was one of the new ones painted blue with designs of yellow, not one of the old ones that looked like a worn-out army jeep. The driver stopped with a jerk, waiting just long enough for them to climb in, and was off with another jerk.

"Quiapo market," they told him as they reached over his shoulder to pay their fare. But they watched land-marks too. Between dodging other jeepneys and winding his way among buses and trucks, and stopping while passengers got off and on, he might forget where two children wanted to go.

"Psst!" whistled Manuel. The jeepney jerked to a stop only a few steps from the entrance to the big covered market. They passed the shops that lined the sidewalk and went into the big, dim building where food was for sale on every side. What fun it was to walk up and down the aisles between tables and booths! Everything smelled delicious. It looked delicious. If the children had not had Mother's list to follow, they would have bought all sorts of interesting things. But they must buy the fish, rice, soap, matches, garlic, bananas, and other everyday things that Mother needed. The children went from booth to booth to find where they could get the most for their money. They remembered that the size of their treat depended on how well they shopped and bargained.

At last the buri bags were full and Manuel's six pesos had been changed into a pile of small red, green, and brown pieces of paper money. Back into Manuel's pocket went a twenty-centavo piece to pay for the jeepney fare home. Then the children bent their heads over the remaining paper money as they counted.

"A peso and sixty centavos!" The children walked from the food market onto the bright sidewalk. "We can get a wonderful treat for that. We won't have to choose between toys and sweets. We can buy both."

Then Nenet stopped smiling for just a just a minute. "When things are going so well for us, I feel more sorry than ever for poor Angie, alone in her house with no fun and no playmates."

Manuel could not think of anything to say.

Up and down the busy sidewalk of Quiapo walked Nenet and Manuel—slowly in front of shops that sold toys or sweets—quickly in front of stores that sold cloth or tools. They turned down side streets, being careful not to lose their way.

"*Tuloy kayo!*"[2] they heard a harsh voice inviting someone to come in. "Tuloy kayo!"

Not having any special place to go, they walked toward the strange voice. They wanted to see who was so eager to have them, or somebody else, come in. They forgot to linger by the woman who sold sugared pili nuts, or the man who sold ice-cream cones, or the shop that sold gaily colored balloons.

"Tuloy kayo!" The voice was inviting them into a store that was all atwitter with a medley of smaller voices. As the children drew nearer, the chirps and chatters were louder.

"A pet shop!" Nenet and Manuel entered and were soon walking between rows of cages. In the low cages, monkeys were scratching, chewing, and chattering. In the middle cages, birds were twittering—little red finches and bigger gray and white lovebirds. In the highest cages, yellow canaries trilled sweet tunes. On the other side of the store were big glass tubs where colored fish swam. And in the center of the shop, with their legs tied to a post, were huge blue and green parrots croaking, "Tuloy kayo" in their harsh voices.

Nenet and Manuel laughed to find who had called

[2]Tuloy kayo (tŭ´ loi kī´ yō)

them into the pet shop. They began reading the price tags.

"Only a peso and twenty centavos for a pair of finches!" said Nenet. The other birds cost more. Manuel fingered the paper money in his pocket. He knew it was more than enough.

"There would need to be a cage," Nenet remembered.

The pet-shop keeper noticed them. "There are some cheap cages made of bamboo strips. They cost only a few centavos."

Nenet and Manuel did not ask each other if the birds were what they wanted to buy as their treat. They knew. It took only a few minutes of bargaining to persuade the pet-shop owner to let them have two finches and a cage for the money they could spend.

"*Salamat,*"[3] the parrot was thanking them while Manuel counted out the paper money. Nenet chose the two small finches that seemed the prettiest and the most friendly.

The two children could scarcely believe what had happened as they walked from the shop with their new pets. They hurried back to the main sidewalk and stopped a jeepney headed for their home.

They hoped the driver would be more careful than usual. Their birds must not be bounced too much. Stepping from the jeepney, they waved gaily at Angie's pale face. She was still peering out of her window over Pedring's store. Angie smiled at the birds—a slow, sad smile.

"After we've taken the groceries home," suggested Manuel, "we can go back and show the birds to Angie."

"Yes," agreed Nenet. "She'll love looking at them. She never has any fun."

"It must be lonesome staying in the house all the time with no playmates," said Manuel.

---

[3]Salamat (sä lä´ mät)

The children did not speak again till they reached home. They were thinking about the same thing. Each was sure what the other was thinking. They knew what to say when their mother came to the top of the stairs to greet them.

"Beautiful!" Mother sounded happy at their choice. "Pet birds are better than toys or sweets! They will look lovely singing in the front window."

"Not in *our* front window!" Manuel looked at Nenet.

She nodded at her brother. Then she said, "They will look lovely in Angie's front window over Pedring's store!"

Then Mother looked even happier than before.

2

The Second Mile

BY TRUMAN DOUGLASS

The great road that stretched for miles in both directions was crowded. Groups of people on foot traveled steadily onward. Donkeys, heavily burdened, passed along. A long train of camels with great, bulky loads high on their backs plodded by. The boy David, standing by the side of the road, watched everything with eager eyes.

"Someday I'll follow the road on and on and on," he thought. "I'll follow it down even to the Great Sea!"

His eyes fell upon a single figure walking alone along the crowded road. "He's a Roman soldier," thought David. "I can tell by the way he's dressed. How I dislike the Romans! If it weren't for them, we Jews would be free again!"

He stared at the Roman soldier, who was almost opposite him now in the road. Suddenly the soldier stopped. He shifted the heavy pack he carried and eased it down to the ground. Then he straightened up again and stood resting a moment, watching the people passing by.

David still stared at him, thinking angry thoughts.

Then, just as the soldier turned to pick up his pack once more, he noticed David nearby.

"Here, boy," he called. "Come here! You will carry this for me!"

David wanted to turn and run, but he did not dare. He knew the Roman law that a Roman soldier could make any Jewish boy or man carry his load for him for one mile.

"But only for one mile!" thought David sullenly as he stepped forward.

The soldier had already turned away and started down the road. He did not even bother looking back to see if David was following him. The soldier knew David would not dare do anything else.

David followed. The pack was heavy, but David was strong. He swung along easily, but his thoughts were angry. He wanted to throw the soldier's pack down and walk away. He wanted to shout his feelings of injustice at the Roman soldier ahead of him. But he could only follow along, keeping his bitter thoughts to himself.

"Well, it's only a mile," he thought. "Just one mile. He can't make me go a step farther. Only one mile."

The words made a sort of song in his mind in time to his steps. "One mile; one mile."

Then as he was plodding along, David suddenly remembered another day when he had walked along this same road. He had gone out to a hillside near the city with some of his friends to listen to a Teacher of whom they had heard.

"What makes me think of Him now?" wondered David with one part of his mind. Another part was still repeating over and over, "One mile; one mile."

"Of course," he remembered. "The Master used those very words. What was it He said about one mile?" He walked on, frowning for a moment before he could

remember. Then he said the words to himself. " 'If anyone forces you to go one mile, go with him two miles.'
That was what He said!" David had not paid very much
attention to it at the time. He remembered now other
things the Master had said. "Love your enemies. Pray for
those who persecute you." Then once more David found
himself repeating the strangest of them all. " 'If anyone
forces you to go one mile, go with him two miles.' Does
He mean—could He mean—like—now?" David puzzled.
"But why? Why should I go more than one mile?"

David was so busy thinking that he did not notice that
the soldier had stopped, and so he almost ran into him.

"You have come a mile," said the soldier. "Give me
the pack."

"I will go on," said David. And he did not know why
he said it. "It has not seemed far. I am not tired."

The Roman soldier stared at him in surprise, and for
the first time David really looked into his face. He saw
that the soldier was very young. He saw too that he was
very, very tired, in spite of the straight, soldierly way in
which he stood.

"You have come a long way," said David.

"Yes," said the other, "a long, weary way."

"Have you far to go?"

"I go to Rome."

"So far!" said David. "Then let me carry your pack
another mile. There is no one here to take it. Another
mile will be nothing."

"You are very kind," said the soldier in amazement.

So they went on, only now the Roman waited for
David and walked beside him along the road. Before long
David found himself talking to the soldier as though
they had known each other for a long time. He told him
all about his home and family. He listened while the soldier talked of his travels in far places. They were so busy

talking that the distance seemed short.

"Tell me," said the soldier at last. "How did it happen that you offered to come this second mile?"

David hesitated. "I hardly know," he said. "It must have been something the Master said." Then he told the soldier what had happened out on the hill and what he remembered of the Master's teachings.

"Strange!" said the soldier thoughtfully. " 'Love your enemies.' That is a hard teaching. I should like to meet this Master."

They had come now to the top of a hill and to the end of the second mile. David looked back along the road toward his home. "I must go back," he said.

The soldier took his pack and shouldered it again. The two clasped hands. "Good-bye . . . friend," said the soldier.

"Good-bye . . . friend," David answered with a smile.

As David strode back along the road, the words of the Master kept running through his mind: "If anyone forces you to go one mile, go with him two miles." And as he repeated the words, he found himself adding with a strange, deep joy: "It works! There's something in it! I walked one mile behind an enemy—I walked the second mile and found a friend!"

3

It's in Your Face

You don't have to tell how you live each day,
You don't have to say if you work or play:
A tried, true barometer serves in the place;
However you live, it will show in your face.

The false, the deceit you bear in your heart
Will not stay inside, where it first got a start,
For sinew and blood are a thin veil of lace;
What you wear in your heart, you wear in your face.

If your life is unselfish, if for others you live,
For not what you get, but for how much you can give,
If you live close to God, in His infinite grace,
You don't have to tell it—it shows in your face.

AUTHOR UNKNOWN

19

4

 Conquering With Kindness

AUTHOR UNKNOWN

I once had a neighbor, a shoemaker, who came to me one day and said, "Neighbor White, I want you to come and lock your geese away!"

"Why," I said, "what are my geese doing?"

"They peck my pigs' ears when they are eating, and drive them from their food. And I will not have it!"

"What can I do?" I asked.

"You must pen them."

"That I have not time to do now," I explained. "If you could wait a short while—"

"If you do not take care of them, I shall!" the shoemaker said in anger. "What do you say, Neighbor White?"

"I cannot take care of them now, but will pay you for any damage they have caused."

"Well," he said, "you will find that a hard thing, I guess."

So off he went, and I heard a terrible squalling among the geese. The next news was that three of them were missing. My children went and found them, mangled and dead, thrown into the bushes. "Now," I said, "all keep still, and let us deal in kindness."

In a few days, the shoemaker's hogs broke into my corn. Before I was able to drive them out, they did much damage to the crop. Nevertheless, I picked up the corn that they had torn down, and fed it to them in the road. In a short while, the shoemaker came up in great haste after them.

"Have you seen anything of my hogs?" he asked.

"Yes, sir. You will find them yonder, eating some corn that they tore down in my field."

"In your field?"

"Yes, sir," I said, "hogs love corn, you know; they were made to eat."

"How much mischief have they done?"

"Oh, not much," I replied.

Well, off he went to look, and estimated the damage to be equal to a bushel and a half of corn.

"Oh, no," I said, "It can't be."

"Yes," said the shoemaker, "and I will pay you every cent of the damage."

"No," I insisted, "you shall pay me nothing. My geese have been a great trouble to you."

The shoemaker blushed and went home. That winter, when we came to settle, the shoemaker once more offered to pay me for my corn. I insisted, however, that he pay me nothing for it, and so after some talk we parted. A few days later, we met on the road and fell into conversation in the most friendly manner.

When I started on, though, he seemed reluctant to move, and so I paused. For a moment both of us were silent. At last he said, "I have something laboring on my mind. Those geese; I killed three of your geese, and I shall never rest until you know how I feel! I am sorry." And tears came to his eyes.

"Oh, well," I replied, "never mind; I suppose my geese were provoking." I never took anything of him for it; but when my cattle broke into his fields after this, he seemed glad because he could show how patient he could be.

"Now," I explained to my children, "have you not seen how you can conquer with kindness where you can conquer in no other way?"

5

 The Hunters

BY W. G. CRISP

Avik[1] and Omak[2] wearily set their packs down on a patch of heather. They wriggled free from the strain of the flat tumplines across their chests and foreheads.

Ah-crawl-ik! Ah-crawl-ik! The cry of the black ducks echoed and reechoed from the low hills across the lake, as their whirring wings carried them in ever-widening circles away from the shore.

The two Inuit youths scarcely glanced up at the flight of ducks. All through their day-long journey over the tundra from the seacoast, the air had been filled with the voices of the waterfowls. The screech of gulls, honk of geese, quack of eider ducks and mallards, and the foolish laugh of the loons came from every small lake and pond.

And always there was the cry of the small black ducks who called out their name. There was no need to look for their long, pointed tail feathers to identify these ducks. *Ah-crawl-ik* was the word by which they were

[1]Avik (ā′ vĭk)
[2]Omak (ō′ măk)

23

known in the language of the Copper Inuit tribes of
Coronation Gulf.

The red disk of the sun now touched the tips of the
farthest hills at midnight. But in spite of the retreating
sun, the brief Arctic summer held on. Whether it would
last for two more days, or two more weeks, no man could
tell. But Avik and Omak knew that two weeks at the
most was all they could expect before the colors faded
from the wildflowers, and the land waited brown and
somber for two full moons before it would be brightened
by the glistening snowdrifts of winter. There would be
gray clouds in the sky and fierce winds sweeping down
from the northern ice fields, bringing rain squalls and
wet snow. Sometimes the sun would break through the
clouds, but there would be little warmth in the sunshine.

For the time being, however, the boys were content to
know it was summer. Avik was setting up their small
tent, not to shelter them from the weather, but because
it would provide them a place where they could escape
from the swarms of mosquitoes.

Omak first covered the kayak[3] with his sleeping robe
to protect it from the rays of the sun. Both boys were
very pleased with the small kayak now that its original
covering of canvas had been replaced with sealskin.

Avik set a match to a few handfuls of moss inside the
tent to drive out the mosquitoes. Then the boys stretched
a piece of netting over the doorway and slept during the
heat of the day.

During the last few days, they had forgotten their
disappointment at not being able to join the caribou
hunters who had set off after a large band of caribou
that had been sighted far to the east of the lakes. They
had been left behind at the camp on the seashore with
the women and children and the old men.

[3]kayak (kī′ ăk)

This year they had hoped to take part in their first real caribou hunt, but their hopes had been dashed when their canoe was wrecked in the falls of Middle River and they had lost their rifles.

Omak had made the kayak from the wreckage of the canoe. And the day after the caribou hunters left the camp, Avik had planned this trip to the inland lakes where they could use the kayak to troll for the big lake trout. None of their band had ever caught them except through the ice in winter. But Avik decided that the big trout must stay in the deep water through the summer. With a long line and a lure carved of polished bone, he was sure he could catch some.

They set the kayak in the water, Avik steadying it as Omak slid into the circular hole in the center and sat with his legs stretched straight out in front of him. The double-bladed paddle flashed in the evening sun as he headed away from shore. He paused every now and then to pay out more line, which he held in his teeth when he resumed paddling. To him it seemed the natural thing to do, for an Inuit's teeth serve him almost like a third hand. And three hands are none too many when you are fishing from a kayak. He knew that if he hooked a fish, he could not hope to pull it into the kayak but would have to paddle for shore.

As Omak's kayak glided across the lake, leaving scarcely a ripple on the smooth waters, his eyes were continually searching the hills around him. But nothing moved except a small flight of ducks and geese and the brown shape of Avik's figure as he climbed the high hill behind the camp. Avik was almost to the top, when suddenly he started to bob up and down and throw his arms in the air.

Omak noticed him at once. He held his paddle with his teeth as he reeled in the fishline with both hands.

And then the kayak cut a deep V in the water as he paddled for the shore at top speed. He knew that Avik's signal meant "Game in sight." It would only mean caribou, but—they had no rifles!

Avik was at the shore when the kayak landed. "Caribou in the valley beyond the hill," he gasped excitedly.

"But we have no rifles—not even a bow and arrow," said Omak.

Avik was speaking rapidly but in a matter-of-fact tone. "The wind is blowing toward the lake. If I make a wide circle, they will head this way when they pick up my scent. They are at the head of a gully leading to the lake, and the hills on either side are tipped with *inyukhuit*[4]—the manlike figures our grandfathers made by piling up stones to frighten the caribou from crossing over the hills."

They looked at each other with broad smiles on their faces. "Sometimes, so we are told, our grandfathers did not even use bows and arrows," muttered Omak. *"Tuki!*[5] *Tuki!* [Hurry! Hurry!]"

Then Avik headed at a brisk trot over the hills, and Omak took the slender ridgepole of the tent and tied his hunting knife to the tip of it.

Omak's heart started to beat rapidly as he climbed into the kayak without Avik's help. It seemed to him that the fragile craft would tip over if he did not hold his breath while he was getting into it.

There was a looped thong of sealskin at the bow, which held the point of the spear while the shaft rested on one side of the circular opening. Omak paddled the kayak with slow, easy strokes of the double-bladed paddle, keeping close under the shadow of the shore so that

[4]inyukhuit (ĭn′ yək hüt)
[5]tuki (tü′ kē)

the nearsighted caribou would see only safety and hope of escape in the clear surface of the lake.

Long minutes passed, which seemed to him like hours. The calls of the ducks and geese seemed far away, but the annoying whine of the mosquitoes was always in his ears. He was in agony as they gorged themselves with his blood, but he dared not brush them off, for any sudden movement might mean the failure of their plan.

Then, above the buzzing of the mosquitoes, he heard an eerie howling from the hills. Avik was imitating the hunting cry of a wolf. Seconds later Omak's sharp eyes spotted brown forms moving along a hillside. And then he could clearly see three caribou trotting down the hollow between the hills—moving with the nervous, stiff-legged gait of their kind.

The scent of man was in their nostrils and the cry of their relentless enemy, the wolf, in their ears. Omak saw the caribou stop, hesitate, mill around in a circle, and then bound together a short distance up the far hillside. Then he could tell that their eyes had glimpsed the dark outlines of the inyukhuit—it seemed the caribou saw these piles of stone as something unnatural which did not belong in these rounded hills. He saw them turn in wild panic, plunge into the water, and start swimming toward the opposite shore of the lake.

Omak forgot the agony of the mosquitoes that were clustered about his face and hands as he whirled the double-bladed paddle and drove the kayak out from the shore. Within a distance of a hundred paces, he caught up with them, for the caribou seemed to him slow swimmers when compared to the speed with which he could paddle the kayak.

Holding the paddle in his left hand, he stabbed at the neck of the closest animal. Its head rose briefly in the air and then fell back. Its body twitched and then was still, floating sideways in the blue water, surrounded by a slowly spreading crimson stain.

Then it was another spurt of paddling, and this time Omak steered the kayak a little too close to the antlered head of the next caribou. As his spear struck home, his kayak was overturned, and for a few seconds he struggled with his head underwater, his lungs bursting, before he managed to right himself.

Then he had to recover his spear, which was floating in the water a few yards away. Once his spear was in his hand again, he was more cautious about how he approached the third animal.

It was all over now except for the slow work of towing the limp carcasses to shore. Avik, who had been watching from shore, was waiting, ready to start on the work of skinning and cutting up the meat.

Before they started skinning, they each ate a slice of the raw liver, just as their grandfathers had done when they drove the caribou herds between the rows of inyukhuit: and killed them with arrows and spears. After that they hardly noticed the attacks of mosquitoes which, attracted by the fresh blood, were landing on them with renewed ferocity.

Avik was suggesting a plan. "You can stay and continue fishing while I return to the camp for help. We have far too much meat here for us to carry alone."

"Ee-la! [Yes!]" said Omak. "And perhaps," he added with a broad grin, "we could have all the meat carried home, and maybe some fresh fish, before the other hunters return."

6

Which Are You?

I watched them tearing a building down,
A gang of men in a busy town;
With a ho-heave-ho and a lusty yell
They swung a beam and the timbers fell.
I asked the foreman, "Are these men skilled,
And the men you'd hire if you had to build?"
He gave a laugh and said, "No indeed!
Just common labor is all I need.
I can easily wreck in a day or two
What builders have taken a year to do!"

And I thought to myself as I went my way,
Which of these roles have I tried to play?
Am I a builder who works with care,
Measuring life by the rule and square?
Am I shaping my deeds to a well-made plan,
Patiently doing the best I can?
Or am I a wrecker, who walks the town,
Content with the labor of tearing down?

AUTHOR UNKNOWN

7

 A Sweet Story*

BY JULIE CLOSSEN KENLY

This is the story of one of the strangest little baby sisters in the world.

Your own baby sister (if you have one) looks much the same as you. The little sister of our story, however, is very different from the older ones in her family. Your mother feeds warm, soothing milk to your little sister. Our story baby starts life on food as sour as vinegar and as hot as red pepper. In a single week, your sister seems to grow hardly at all. In one week, this tiny stranger is a thousand times heavier than when she was born. Your baby sister is a helpless little thing for a long, long time. But in three weeks this other baby is doing the housework in her home, and is already forty years old as her family reckons age.

Who is this strange and wonderful little sister? It is Baby Bee, and this is her story.

BEGINNING DAYS

Baby Bee began her life as a mere speck of jelly sealed up inside an eggshell. The egg was shaped like a

30

banana—a very, very small banana. Not even a micro-scope would have shown you anything inside this tiny, bluish white speck, yet God had put there the power to make another bee of the same pattern as the mother who laid the egg.

Mother Bee laid this egg at the bottom of a six-sided cup of wax. Alongside it were hundreds of little sister eggs, each in its own separate cup. Together these cups formed the cells of a honeycomb. Mother Bee had a harder time laying her eggs than Mother Hen, who had only to lay hers in a bed of straw. Mother Bee had to put a dab of glue on the downward end of each of her little eggs so that it would stick to the floor of its cell. This done, the egg stuck straight up, for all the world like a light bulb in a socket.

From time to time, after the egg was laid, along would come a bee nurse. She would stick her head into the little cup to see how things were coming along. Through the transparent shell of the egg she could see Baby Bee gradually putting herself together. First one part and then another would form inside the egg.

Did you ever see an egg with enough sense to know when to stand up and when to lie down? This one knew. Baby Bee's egg stayed up on end until a few hours before it hatched. Then it lay down on its side!

This told the nurse bee that the moment was near for the egg to hatch. Carefully she put a droplet of bee food near the point of the cell where the egg was attached. When Baby Bee finally tore through the shell, she found her dinner waiting for her. It was a very unusual dinner called royal jelly, which resembled sweetened condensed milk, but tasted as sour as gooseberries and stung like red pepper. Where do you suppose it came from? It spurted out of little openings in the nurse bee's forehead.

For a week her nurse continued to stuff Baby Bee with food. And how she grew! We humans think that we know how to feed babies to make them grow fast. Yet bees can feed their babies so well that it was possible for Baby Bee to gain over a thousand times her weight in one week. Think of a human baby, weighing eight pounds at birth, and one week later weighting as much as a large farm tractor. Perhaps it is better that we do not know how to feed our baby sisters with such effectiveness.

You must not imagine that Baby Bee looked like the bees that we know. In fact, she did not look as much like an adult bee as we do. She had no separate head, body, or legs. Instead, she was all in one piece, and in the shape of a sausage. A very homely and unattractive sausage it was, too, with white satiny skin and a little black head. In this stage of her life, Baby Bee was known as a larva.

At first, Baby Bee was very happy as a larva. She had more rich food than she could possibly eat, and no work to do. After a few days of heavy stuffing, however, the little white grub began to feel very uncomfortable. The baby skin in which she was hatched became tighter and tighter, till finally it went *pop*! There she was, with a new and roomier coat that had been growing all along under her old skin.

By this time, Baby Bee had grown so fat that she crowded the walls of her cell. This told the nurse bee that the baby was ready for the sleep that would turn her into adult. At once the nurse bee made a cap of yellowish wax to seal the cell. With it she mixed various sorts of bee trash to make sure that it would be loose enough for air to get through.

BABY BEE GROWS UP

As soon as Baby Bee found that her door was closed, she began to do another wonderful thing. She began to spin herself a cocoon—a delicate little sleeping bag of fine web. She had now become a pupa and was about to undergo a miraculous change in appearance.

Little by little, as Baby Bee slept, her shape changed. The little sausage divided itself into three parts. One part became a head, another part became a chest, or thorax, and the third part became a stomach, or abdomen. From her head emerged little feelers called antennae. From her chest sprouted six legs, which she folded over her breast. On and on went the changes until a whole bee had developed, still sound asleep in its cell. At this point, Baby Bee looked like a tiny toy bee, carved from pure ivory.

Now God began to paint this little ivory bee. First the tips of Baby's antennae began to grow darker. Then came the head and eyes, the eyes turning first pink and then black. Last of all, the thorax and abdomen were painted in stripes of bronze and black to match those of Baby's mother. As her coloring neared completion, Baby's body began to twitch in small jerks and shivers.

Then came the last day of her miraculous sleep. Baby's wings quivered and then folded under her. She turned over onto her stomach and began to scrape with her new legs and to bite with her new jaws. Soon there was a hole in the cap of her cell and she was free of her enclosure.

The first thing she did outside her cell was to rub her nose and straighten her velvety fur. She was beginning to feel hungry. A walk across the comb brought her to an uncapped cell of honey. It was the first taste she had of something sweet. How pleasant it was!

For the next two days, all Baby Bee did was eat and comb her fur. Her eyesight was poor, and her intelligence was not fully developed. Nor could she yet use her wings. These two days were the last of her babyhood.

Unlike our baby sister, in just one week this little bee was old enough to be trusted with her share of the work about the hive. She had to take on the care of the brood comb and to become, in her turn, a nurse for other baby bees. Now from her forehead ran fountains of royal jelly. On her faithful little shoulders fell the dusting of the hive, the making of wax, and the building of combs.

At ten days old, our little bee (a baby no longer) had her first great adventure. Out of the gloomy darkness of the hive she crawled, to take her first flight into the outside world. How wonderful it must have been to see the blue sky and white clouds, and the colorful flowers surrounding her hive! How excited she was to smell all those sweet perfumes!

At three weeks, our little bee was as old to her family as a person of forty seems to us. She was strong and intelligent, and able to turn her jaws to any sort of work. She lived in a clean, well-built house under a reliable bee government. If she were able to talk, she might have told you that there are many things worse than the life of a bee.

*Originally title "Baby Bee" © 1935, D. Appleton-Century Co., Inc. 1963, Henry Clossen Kenly. Reprinted by permission from Hawthorn Properties (Elsevier-Dutton Publishing Co., Inc.)

8

James Dulin's Bargain

BY RUTH CHESTERFIELD

"Hello, Dulin! Have you heard the news?" cried neighbor Shillebah, stopping his horse and hailing a young man who was returning from his day's work with a hoe over his shoulder.

"I've heard nothing special," James answered cheerily.

"Well, there is something special to hear. A gold mine has been discovered near Newburyport! I've just come from there, and that's all anyone can talk about."

"They've been a good while finding it," James observed dryly.

"I see you think it's a hoax, but I'm being completely honest with you."

"No doubt of that—at least, no doubt you think you are. It just seems to me that the land around Newburyport should have been pretty much dug over by now."

"That's just what I thought, but here's the proof! What do you think of this?" Mr. Shillebah pulled a carefully wrapped sample of the precious ore from his jacket pocket.

"I declare, it looks like the real thing, doesn't it?" James stated. "There's no mistake about its having been found in Newburyport, is there?"

"Not a bit, and what's more, the talk is that what's been found so far is only the first trace of a mother lode that will make rich men of half the town!"

"That could well be!" exclaimed James, who was becoming more enthusiastic by the moment. "And who knows, we could be on top of a gold mine this very minute! I don't see why New Hampshire is not as likely to have one as Massachusetts."

"Neither do I. The soil can't be so very different." And pocketing his specimen, Mr. Shillebah chirruped to his horse and rode off to spread the news still further.

James Dulin walked the rest of the way to his small cottage more slowly than usual. He was thinking about what he had heard and was so lost in his thoughts that he almost passed his own door without realizing it. His wife, however, who was watching at the kitchen window for his arrival, spied him as he went walking by and called out gaily, "Why, James, where are you going?"

"Oh, I didn't notice!" he said with a start. "I was thinking of the news that Mr. Shillebah brought from Newburyport. They've discovered a gold mine down there."

"That's a likely story, isn't it now?" his wife replied laughingly.

"It's true enough; I've seen the gold myself," James returned huffily, quite forgetting his own disbelief of a few minutes earlier.

"I'm sorry. I thought you were joking," his wife apologized.

"No, I'm quite serious, Nancy," he continued, beginning to tell all the details of his visit with Mr. Shillebah.

"Wouldn't it be odd if people came flocking to New

Hampshire in search of gold instead of going to California?" his wife concluded. "But for now, sit down to your supper before your pancakes get any colder."

James obeyed, though it was clear that he could not bring himself to think about anything save Mr. Shillebah's news. At one point during the evening, after a long silence, he suddenly exclaimed, "What if I should find gold on my own land?"

"I've no doubt you will," Nancy answered.

"What! Do you really think so?" James asked in surprise.

But when he realized his wife was not serious, he became provoked with her. Silence followed, and the evening turned into the most unpleasant one they had shared during the six months of their married life.

From that time on, the gold fever ran high with James Dulin. As more and more stories about the gold find at Newburyport poured in, he could think of nothing but jumping into a fortune. The old way of earning a living seemed altogether too slow, and now that he had begun to dream of castles in the air, the Dulin's little cottage built on the solid foundation of the earth seemed hardly enough to be content with.

One evening as he was returning home with a spade resting on his shoulder and his head quite filled with imaginings, a woodchuck ran across his path. James gave chase and in a moment was almost upon it.

"Now I've got you, sir!" he cried, raising his spade. But the woodchuck made a last desperate scramble and dived into its hole. Vexed, James began to dig into the burrow, intent on destroying the pest. And then, as he dug, he saw something glittering in the dirt on his spade!

His heart gave a bound! Trembling, he picked up the shining substance and found that it looked almost exactly like the gold ore that Mr. Shillebah had shown him. It was almost more than poor James could bear. He sank to the ground, and it was a good while before he was able to calm himself.

Then the thought occurred to him that the precious metal might not be found in that spot only. So he took his spade and sank it into the earth in a number of different places, and with nearly every spadeful he found the precious ore! But it was growing dark and he could not see to dig much longer, so he filled his pockets and covered up all traces of his work, planning to return the next morning.

Then he realized for the first time that, although he had no doubt discovered a mine, it was not on his own property! It was on Mr. Shillebah's land! He was, therefore, no better off for his discovery.

His spirits, which had been raised to the highest just moments before, now sank to the lowest. He brooded over the problem as he walked slowly home. Not even his wife's cheerful conversation could win a smile from him that evening. The Dulin home was becoming, not a place of joy, but a place of discontent.

Several days passed, during which time James made many trips to Mr. Shillebah's pasture where he would worry and scheme about the treasure he longed to possess. At last he decided he would say nothing of his discovery but would try to buy the land and become owner of the mine.

Having decided this, he went to Mr. Shillebah and made what seemed to be a fair offer. Mr. Shillebah, however, agreed to sell the pasture only if James would take the whole parcel, which included an additional one hundred acres of as scrubby, barren, and rocky soil as could be found. Of course the price had to be raised to cover the extra land. This was certainly more than James could afford, but what, after all, were a few added dollars where a gold mine was in question? So the bargain was made, although James had to mortgage his farm for security.

Now that the matter was settled, he could no longer keep the secret from his wife. She was busy ironing when he returned from Mr. Shillebah's. "Nancy! Nancy!" he cried. "Throw away your flatiron; you needn't work any more. You're a rich woman now!"

"*Me*, a rich woman? Well, I guess I'll keep ironing until I see the money come in," she said, supposing that her husband was joking.

"No, I'm quite serious. Listen to me!" Then, taking her hand in his, James told her the whole story from the discovery of the gold to the bargain he had just completed.

"Did Mr. Shillebah know there was gold on that land?" Nancy asked.

"Of course not!" her husband exclaimed. "Do you think he would have sold it to me if he did?"

"But, James, its seems to me you should have told him," his wife continued.

"Told him! That *is* a good one! He had the same chance to make the discovery that I had."

"But he didn't make it."

"That was unfortunate for him and fortunate for me."

"It was, James, and for that reason I'd go and offer to share the profits with him now."

"Surely you're not serious!" shouted James. "A good deal you know about business matters, don't you?"

"No, I know very little about such things; perhaps that is why I cannot think that this is an honest bargain."

"So you accuse me of dishonesty, do you?"

"Is it doing as you would be done by, James?"

"Oh, come now, so you are going to preach. Well, I

must be going. I want to be in Boston tonight to have my metal tested. Get a change of clothes ready for me!"

When James Dulin reached the assayer's office, he was kept waiting a long while, for there was a large crowd there on the same errand as himself. Many besides James had been bitten by the same gold bug as he. But his turn came at last.

"So this is your specimen, Mr. Dulin," stated the assayer, taking it in his hand. "No need to test it, I'm afraid. It is not gold—it is pyrite, or fool's gold as some call it."

"Not gold?" gasped James

"No, it is nothing but sulfur and iron—a very common mistake. You are the fourth person who has brought me pyrite today, believing it to be gold."

The assayer turned away, and James, seeing that he was dismissed, took his leave with a heart heavier than the metal he had craved. All his misdeeds of the past while came to his mind. His greed, his dishonesty, and the angry words he had spoken to Nancy—all were laid bare before him. With shame he thought of the contented, happy state he had been in before he had caught sight of the Newburyport gold.

His first words as he entered his house were, "Nancy, I am a ruined man! We have lost our farm and gained nothing. It was not gold that I found! How could I have been so blind? If only I had it to do over again!"

Then she who had been his accuser became his comforter. "I am relieved of a burden!" she cried, throwing her arms about him. "I thought you had returned to ask me to share ill-gotten riches, but it is only honest poverty."

And James Dulin is not the only man who has become obsessed with riches and sought them by dishonest means, only to find not gold, but fool's gold.

The Daisy

Not worlds on worlds in phalanx deep
 Need we to prove a God is here;
The daisy, fresh from winter's sleep,
 Tells of His hand in lines as clear.

For who but He that arched the skies
 And pours the dayspring's living flood,
Wondrous alike in all He tries,
 Could rear the daisy's purple bud?

He made its cup, its wiry stem;
 Its fringed border nicely spin,
And cut the gold-embossed gem
 That, set in silver, gleams within;

Then flung it, unrestrained and free,
 O'er hill and dale and desert sod,
That man, where'er he walks, may see,
 In every step, the stamp of God.

J. M. Good

10

 The Sacrifice

BY ELIZABETH WAGLER

PART I

Twelve-year-old Ralph Morely felt elated that fine June morning. With a heavy roll of barbed wire slung over his shoulder and a hammer tucked into his belt, he followed his father across the summer pasture.

As he hitched his burden up higher and lengthened his stride, he thought of Molly, the fawn-colored heifer calf Father had brought home for him the day before. Ralph had big plans for her. "In two years Molly will have a calf," he thought to himself. "If it's a heifer, we'll keep it and have two milk cows. If it's a bull, I'll sell it and buy another heifer—"

"Whoa-a, there!" Father's warning prevented Ralph from walking head-on into the old barbed wire fence at the back of the pasture.

"Were you, by any chance, dreaming about a herd of Jersey cows?" asked Father with an understanding twinkle in his eyes.

"Yes," admitted Ralph with a grin. "If Molly has a heifer calf, we'll have two cows and . . ."

"Not so fast," cautioned Father, digging a handful of fencing staples from his pocket. "It takes years to build up a herd. And if we don't fix this fence today, we won't even have Molly for long. Now, could you start unwinding that roll?"

They worked companionably for about an hour, replacing broken strands, stretching a new wire across the top of the fence, and straightening leaning fence posts.

"Hello, there, Morely! Fixing the fence, I see."

Father and Ralph straightened up to see Mr. Whitney, whose property bordered theirs, strolling toward them.

Father took the staples out of his mouth. "Hello, Mr. Whitney. Yes, I just bought a calf for my boy here, so we're trying to make sure she'll stay home. It's a fine day, isn't it?"

Mr. Whitney ignored the comment about the weather. He frowned at Ralph, who was resting his arms gingerly on the top strand of barbed wire. "Well, you'd better keep that animal off my property," he warned. "I dislike animals. Other folks' dogs drag my garbage around; cats chase the chipmunks away; and cows will eat my garden."

"Well, we'll certainly try to see to it that our calf doesn't eat your garden," Father quickly assured him.

"Ha!" snorted Mr. Whitney. "Just remember," he shook his forefinger at them, "if that calf ever steps on my property, I'll shoot it!" At that, he turned and stalked away.

Ralph and his father watched his retreat in silence. When he was out of their hearing, Ralph burst out, "Of all things! Why should he be so upset just because we want to raise a calf? He'd better not shoot Molly."

"Take it easy, son," cautioned Father, gazing across

the pasture after Mr. Whitney. "Our neighbor is a very unhappy man, and we should do what we can to help him. I must admit, though," he went on, "that sometimes it seems difficult to help people like Mr. Whitney. We will just have to continue to pray for him and show the love of Christ by our actions. Hopefully, we'll be able to keep the calf in our field."

The summer days glided by. Molly stayed in the field where she belonged. Ralph spent most of his spare time with her. He brushed her coat until it shone. He taught her to lead on a short rope. When he checked the fence, Molly followed at his heels like an overgrown puppy, playfully trying to catch his shirt tail with her rough tongue.

Sometimes, while checking the fence alongside Mr. Whitney's property, Ralph would pause and watch him working in his garden. Although Father made every effort to be friendly whenever he met Mr. Whitney, the older man remained gruff and did not return Father's greetings. Ralph doubted that he would ever change. It seemed like no amount of kindness or love would change such a grumpy old man.

September came. One morning, just as Ralph was seating himself at the table for breakfast, the phone rang. He listened as Father spoke into the receiver.

"Hello?"

"Yes, Mr. Whitney. How are you today?"

There was a long pause. Ralph could hear a loud voice cracking on the other end of the phone. Father's face grew sober as he listened.

When the voice finally subsided, Father replied quietly, "Thank you for calling, Mr. Whitney. We'll be right over." Slowly he replaced the receiver and turned to face his son.

"What happened?" Ralph asked apprehensively.

Father's eyes were full of sympathy. "Molly was in Mr. Whitney's garden . . . and he shot her. I'm sorry, Ralph."

Ralph's shoulders slumped. "Oh, no!" he groaned. He dropped his head between his hands and stared hard at his plate.

"She was only an animal, Ralph." Father rested a hand on Ralph's shoulder. "Sometimes the Lord asks us to give up something we prize in order to accomplish His purposes."

It was hard for Ralph to see what good Molly's death could accomplish. Father went on, "Perhaps this sacrifice will open the door of communication with Mr. Whitney. He will expect us to retaliate or at least be angry. But we must show only love and forgiveness. Let's pray for guidance before we leave to get the calf."

A short time later they pulled into the Whitney's yard. The dead calf lay next to the garden. Father backed the pickup close to the body, and he and Ralph got out. Ralph, his hands stuffed deep into his pockets, stood looking at his pet, while Father started toward Mr. Whitney.

"Told you I'd shoot if that animal ever came over here!" Mr. Whitney's voice boomed across the lawn. "She was in my garden helping herself to the cabbage," he continued loudly. "All that work I put into my garden, and some silly animal destroys it in a few minutes. Sure is disgusting!" He waved his arms agitatedly.

Father faced the angry man. "I'm sorry about the damage she did. I'm sure it must be frustrating. We have more cabbage in our garden than we can use. We will replace what she has eaten, or pay you if you prefer. Did she destroy anything else?"

Mr. Whitney, in the act of replying, caught sight of Ralph's sad countenance. He swallowed quickly and turned his head in the direction of his garden. "Ah, no. I

don't think she did anything else," he admitted in a
milder tone.

"We want to be sure to pay you for any damage she
may have caused. I don't know how she got through the
fence. We've been checking it regularly. But we must
have overlooked some weak spot."

Mr. Whitney made no reply, and he watched in
silence as Father and Ralph loaded Molly's carcass into
the pickup box.

Brushing his hands on his trousers, Father
addressed Mr. Whitney. "I think we'll go home and
butcher now. I'll be over shortly to settle up."

PART II

In the following days, Ralph thought often about
what had happened. Had anything been gained by the
death of his pet?

Mr. Whitney had refused to accept any payment for
the damage to his garden. He had even attempted an
apology over the fence to Father one afternoon. "I acted
a little too hastily," he had stammered. "Maybe you can
get the boy another calf."

It did seem as though he had softened a bit, Ralph
had to admit.

One day, several weeks after Molly's death, Father
assigned Ralph an unexpected task. "Mr. Whitney has a
lame back, and he asked if you would split some wood for
him. I'm pleased that he felt free to ask for our help. He
would never have done that before this business with
Molly. You go over and do a good job for him, Ralph."

Ralph, not sure what to expect, set out for the
Whitneys. He had been splitting wood for over an hour
when Mr. Whitney came hobbling across the yard
toward him.

"That's enough to last all week," the old man said. "You needn't do any more."

"I'll just finish up these last few pieces," offered Ralph.

"Very well; it will sure be nice to have it done. My back really bothers me in this cold weather." Mr. Whitney seated himself painfully on a large chunk of wood and watched until Ralph was finished.

Then, with the help of a cane, he slowly got to his feet. "Come into the house, and my wife will make you a cup of hot chocolate," he offered.

"Oh, thanks, Mr. Whitney," Ralph said, "but"—he glanced at his watch—"I have to go home and do chores before it gets dark."

"Well, then, take this," and Mr. Whitney reached into his pocket and held out a crumpled bill.

Ralph gasped, "Oh, ten dollars is far too much, Mr. Whitney! I didn't work long enough for this. I can't take it. You don't have to pay me anything."

"Take it," Mr. Whitney said gruffly, thrusting the money into Ralph's reluctant palm. "Save it. Buy another calf next spring."

The winter passed quickly, and soon it was spring again. On a bright, sunny day in early May, Ralph, pliers in hand, walked along the pasture fence, checking the wires. At his heels trotted Molly Too.

When boy and calf reached the back of the pasture, Mr. Whitney, who had been pruning his raspberry bushes, came over and leaned against a fence post. He lifted his straw hat and smoothed back his gray hair while he looked the animal over. "Looks like you've got yourself a fine calf, young man," he offered, replacing his hat.

"Yes, sir," Ralph agreed.

"Well, you take good care of her," Mr. Whitney

advised with a smile as he started back to his raspberry patch.

As Ralph watched the old man ambling across the field, he shook his head wonderingly. "Well, Molly Too," he finally stated, "let's see that you stay on our side of the fence. I think one sacrifice has been enough."

11

 Wanderers of the Sea

AUTHOR UNKNOWN

"They that go down to the sea in ships,
that do business in great waters;
these see the works of the LORD,
and his wonders in the deep."

PSALM 107:23, 24

Icebergs are wanderers of the sea. Every spring as we on the land are beginning to watch for spring flowers and birds, sailors along our more northern shipping routes are on the lookout for these great mountains of ice which start to drift southward. They are very beautiful sights with their rainbow colors, but the sailors realize the danger of running into them and go many miles out of their way to avoid them.

Where do these immense floating islands have their birth? Most of them come from Greenland's great ice fields. In this cold country, snow does not melt from one year to the next, so Greenland is almost entirely covered with a sheet of ice and snow more than a mile thick in places. These ice fields, or glaciers, move imperceptibly seaward, where the land slopes into the ocean. On reaching the sea, their leading edges form high cliffs or shelves which are pushed very slowly from the land.

Each day these shelves are pushed a littler farther out to sea, and each day they sink a little deeper into the water. Waves beat against them until large caves are worn in their sides. Eventually great cracks begin to cut their way through the ice. Suddenly, with a roar like thunder, a greąt mass breaks off and goes crashing into the water. This is the way an iceberg is born to begin a southward journey that may last six or eight months.

Icebergs are of many different sizes, from the small ones called growlers to great masses a mile or more across. They may be as high as three hundred feet above water, but that is only a small fraction of their real size. Only about one-eighth of an iceberg shows above the surface.

In the daytime or in clear weather, icebergs can be sights of great beauty. Their pale green surfaces are shaded brilliant blue in spots. The great caves that are worn in their sides by the waves reflect a deep purple. At dawn and at sunset they are changed to gold and rose. As they drift along, sparkling in the sunlight, they look like beautiful ice castles. At night they glow with a strange white light.

New icebergs are being formed constantly. Each year, a great parade starts on its way early in the spring, following the south-flowing ocean currents off Greenland. In the months of April, May, and June, they reach the major northern shipping routes. The largest bergs may travel two thousand miles before they disappear, but they are never found farther than four hundred miles south of the Canadian island of Newfoundland. Coast Guard cutters and planes are kept busy watching for them and sending out warnings to vessels.

As they float southward, they are warmed by the rays of the sun, and gradually they melt in the warmer ocean water. From time to time, great pieces break from their sides to drop into the water with a loud crash. It is dangerous for vessels to draw near them because huge splinters can fall at any time.

Icebergs are often surrounded by thick layers of fog, which can make it difficult for sailors to see and avoid them. Fog may even hide icebergs completely from sight. They have caused many shipwrecks and much loss of life.

An iceberg is the most dangerous when it begins to melt more rapidly beneath the surface than above. It can become top-heavy and turn directly over in the water. When this happens, there is a hoarse roar followed by a huge crash and giant waves.

As an iceberg melts, rivers of water begin to flow down its sides. Lakes form on its level surfaces, and great cracks appear. Finally, with an explosion like thunder, it bursts. Pieces of ice are thrown far and wide. These soon melt in the warm waters, and the iceberg is no more.

12

 Composition Theme

The Better Way

Submit to the guidance of those who are wiser than yourselves, and become wise by the wisdom of those who have gone before you.

SARGENT

13

 Lito Find His Way

AUTHOR UNKNOWN

Lito leaned on the bamboo fence that marked the yard around the small wooden church with its roof of dried palm leaves. He rested his arms by leaning on the fence instead of his crutches for a few minutes.

He was glad he had dared to come as far as the church fence today. Yesterday he had stood across the rutted road to watch the boys and girls under the big mango tree in the churchyard. People, cars, and carabao[1] on the road kept shutting off his view of what was going on.

Now he was so near the Bible class that he could see the big, colored pictures the teacher was showing. The children called her Miss Naomi. She did not belong to their city but came in the big red bus every morning to teach vacation Bible school. Lito, even from across the road, liked her soft voice and her friendly smile. Now, leaning on the fence, he could hear the stories she was telling about the pictures.

Lito hoped nobody would notice him and start teasing him about his ragged clothes, or his twisted and useless

[1]carabao (kăr ə bou′)

53

leg, or his skinny dog, or his father who wasted time and pesos on cockfights. They might tease him because he had never been to school and could not read or write, even though he was old enough to be in fourth or fifth grade. The children in Lito's barrio[2] seemed to delight in finding new and cruel ways to show he was not good enough to play with them. Lito was afraid that these children would treat him in the same way.

Lito shifted his weight and leaned more heavily on the fence of bamboo poles. It creaked. The teacher and children turned to see what made the noise. Lito picked up his crutches and hobbled away.

"Come back!" called Miss Naomi. "Come into the churchyard with us! Do not run away!"

But Lito's crutches kept tapping on the road that was hard in the brief dry season that comes to the Philippines in March, April, and May. His crutches tapped and tapped until he reached his own nipa hut, the smallest and dirtiest and shakiest in the barrio. Some said there was no poorer hut in the whole province, and perhaps they spoke the truth.

It was the next day before Lito limped quietly toward the church again. He waited till the boys and girls were all there so that none of them would be on the road to make fun of him. This time he did not lean on the fence even to rest his arms. He stood close to the fence, leaning on his crutches.

He could see the picture Miss Naomi was holding in front of the children, who sat in a semicircle before her. He could hear her story. It was about a very kind and good man named Jesus, who loved children, animals, poor people, sick people—everybody.

"See the lame boy in the picture!" Miss Naomi was holding up a brightly colored picture showing a boy with

---

[2]barrio (bä′ rē ō)

crutches. "That little lame boy knew that Jesus loved him. He knew . . . "

But Lito missed the next words because of the noise of his own crutches and good foot as he hobbled nearer to the gate of the churchyard. He stood by the bamboo gate listening to the song the boys and girls were singing.

> Long ago the little children
> Gathered close at Jesus' knee,
> For His kindly smile said gently,
> "I love them and they love Me."

> Come and listen to the story,
> Friend of children still is He;
> Listen then and whisper softly,
> "I love Him and He loves me."

Lito never knew how it happened. He did not plan to walk through that church gate. But there he was in his rags, leaning against the very mango tree under which the children were sitting in their clean Bible school clothes. And most surprising of all, he was singing with the children as they sang their song a second time: "I love them and they love Me."

He saw Miss Naomi look at him and whisper to the girl who sat next to him. But to Lito's great surprise, he was not afraid. He sang through the second verse with the children: "I love Him and He loves me."

"Oh, Lito!" said Miss Naomi, for the girl next to her had told her his name. "You have a lovely voice."

"You sing better than any of us," said one of the boys. "I wish you'd come to Bible school every day and help us sing."

"Yes, yes," said the children. "We want you to come!"

Lito looked at the boys. Weren't they going to tease

him? He looked at the girls. Wouldn't they giggle at his tattered clothes and mended crutches? No, they were smiling at him. "We want you, Lito," they seemed to say. He wondered if it was church or Miss Naomi's stories about Jesus that made the difference.

"Let's sing some more—with Lito to help us," said Miss Naomi.

Then Lito forgot that he had never been to school because of his crutches, and shabby clothes, and the cost of schoolbooks. He forgot that this was the first time he had ever dared hobble inside the bamboo fence of the churchyard. He forgot that he was the boy that nobody liked and everybody teased. Now Lito was a boy who was wanted. He was a boy who could help the others with their singing. Lito hobbled closer to Miss Naomi and sat down in the circle with the other boys and girls.

After class, Lito went home singing in time to the tapping of his crutches: "Come and listen to the story . . ."

He told his tired mother, his thin brothers and sisters, and his lazy father all that he had heard at Bible school. He was happy that they let him go back to the church the next day after and on and on as long as vacation Bible school lasted. He was still happier when they came to the program on the last day of school to hear him sing with his new friends.

But he was happiest of all when they decided to go to church with him one Sunday—and kept on going Sunday after Sunday.

14

 My Childhood in Scotland

AS TOLD BY JEAN YOUNG TO E. WAGLER

When I was a child in Scotland forty years ago, it seemed as though the sky was blue, the sun shone, and the heather bloomed every day. I know this is not a true picture, for we experienced hard winters and gloomy rainy spells; but it is the joyful memories which follow us through the years, while the melancholy scenes fade into the background.

Our little mining village of Greengairs was located halfway between Edinburgh and Glasgow in the Southern Uplands of Scotland. Most of our friends' fathers worked in "the pit." They would come home at night coated with black coal dust. We were always glad our father wasn't a coal worker, because we didn't have to scrape mud from his boots every night as the miners' children did. Our father was an engineer who maintained the machinery in the local brickworks.

Our house was the end unit in a row of four adjoining dwellings. It was made of local brick and topped with a slate roof. Each cottage had one door and two windows. All the houses in our section of Greengairs were owned by a Captain Watts. The captain lived in a big gray house on the hill. As children, we often sat on the stone dyke[1] surrounding his grounds and watched his flock of peacocks strut back and forth across the spacious lawn.

Behind the cottage, my mother kept a little garden plot where she raised vegetables and herbs. In front of the buildings, the women in the row planted flowers, especially climbing roses.

The inside of our house was divided into two rooms: a large front room and a tiny back room. The front room was a true living room. In it we cooked, ate, worked, played, and slept. Our beds were cubicles built into the wall, several feet off the floor. My mother stored her laundry baskets, washtubs, and other utensils in the space under her bed. My father kept his tools and gun under the bed I shared with my sister. At the sides of the cubicles hung stiffly starched white lace curtains which we drew shut for privacy. The appearance of these curtains was important to my mother, and grief befell anyone who tore or rumpled them.

[1]dyke (dīk): a stone wall or fence

My brothers slept in the tiny back room. It contained a large wooden wardrobe where we stored all our clothes.

Mattresses? We never heard of them! We slept very comfortably on straw or feather ticks. Every spring we dismantled our beds and took the boards outside, where we gave them a thorough scrubbing before leaving them against the wall to dry. Everyone in the row knew, then, when others were doing their spring cleaning.

The grate[2] dominated the front room. A huge black affair, it had a high luster that was maintained by constant rubbing with a lump of black lead. Over the fire we heated all our water, cooked our meals, and warmed our toes in the winter.

The water bucket occupied a special place behind the front door. One faucet in the yard served four families. It was a never-ending chore to keep that bucket filled with fresh water. A little tin dipper hung from a nail above the bucket. Repeatedly my mother told us, "Now, when you take a drink, don't take any more than you need, and don't you ever throw what you don't drink back into the bucket!" I'm still thrifty with water.

Washday was a busy day for all. It took many trips to the faucet to fill Mother's big cast-iron kettle. In summer, the boys rose before dawn to build a fire in the yard for heating the water. Mother washed on a scrub board in a big wooden tub. Often the other ladies in the row joined her and they would visit while they worked. When we came home from school, we helped turn the hand wringer. If my mother was particularly tired, she let us scrub the socks. Having rolled up our sleeves and wearing big rubber aprons, we had a splashing good time. We saved the bedding and table linens for the laundry man who came around every two weeks.

[2]grate: a fireplace fitted with iron grates for cooking

We dreaded rainy and winter washdays. Then we would come home to a steamy kitchen crowded to bursting with washtubs and piles of clothes. There was hardly room to move. And we almost always had soup on washdays, that being the least time-consuming dish to prepare.

We fared well on meat, potatoes, and vegetables. For breakfast we ate oatmeal porridge, and eggs from our own hens. Sausage came in a block from which we sliced off pieces to fry. Mother made pan bread, with a black, almost-burnt crust on top and a very light crust underneath. "Eat the dark crust; 'twill make you grow," she used to say to remind us not to hide our crusts behind our plates.

A never-ending stream of vendors traveled the streets in those days. The milkman came around every morning with a wooden barrel sitting on a horse-drawn wagon. We ran out with our pint or quart containers, and he opened a little tap to let the cold, frothy milk bubble into them. From him we also brought cream and butter. The blast of a horn announced the arrival of the butcher's van. We bought meat three times a week. We had no refrigerators or freezers, of course. The baker visited too, with a tantalizing array of bread, scones, London buns, and tea cakes. The coal man kept the coal-shed filled; the paraffin[3] man supplied fuel for our lamps, and every now and then a fish vender offered fresh fish at our doorstep.

At mealtimes we each found a big cup of buttermilk by our plates. That was our favorite drink. The buttermilk came from the farm down the glen.[4] We enjoyed taking time out from our work to go scampering down to the farm, covered buckets swinging from our arms. A

[3]paraffin: kerosene
[4]glen: a small valley

shortcut to the farm led over a stone dyke and across a pasture where Ayrshire cows grazed contentedly. As long as the cows didn't come too near, we chose this route, but we didn't quite trust their pointed horns.

At the farm, the Irishman who lived in the little bothy[5] at the end of the byre[6] filled our pails and offered us a tinny[7] of fresh buttermilk before we started home again.

"Down the glen," that was our playground. On a summer day the whole gang skipped and ran and whooped down the hill to the burn[8] in the glen. We spent hours splashing and wading in that burn. Old jam jars made good minnow traps. The little fish swam into them, and we happily carried home our catch and kept them in a jar of water for a few days. Then our mother would say, "I think you'd better take the wee fishes back to the burn now."

Like all little girls, we played house with our home-made stocking dolls, in crude shelters of leaves, twigs, and moss. We gathered bouquets of pink, purple, and white wild heather, and bluebells to decorate our make-believe houses.

What toys we had were homemade. Every Scottish child possessed a cleek[9] and a gird.[10] Our father made the cleek with a hook in the end. The gird came from a wooden barrel. (Potatoes, oranges, and salted fish all came in wooden barrels, so there were plenty to go around.) We rolled our girds for miles, it seemed, along the roads, up and down the hills, and around corners.

[5]bothy (both´ ē): a farm hand's apartment
[6]byre (bir): a cow stable or shed
[7]tinny: an aluminum mug
[8]burn: a brook
[9]cleek: a stick for rolling a hoop
[10]gird: a barrel hoop

The boys also made kites using the barrel hoops for the main frame. We skipped rope and played marbles or chuckies.[11] The chuckies we made from clay and baked in the oven at home. A whip and a peery[12] were popular toys. The wooden peery was painted in brightly colored rings. We wrapped the string of the whip around it and gave a pull to get the peery going. Then we whipped it and whipped it to keep it whirling. The colors blended into a pretty design.

The boys played rounders. It was much like baseball except that they used a rather flat bat and called the bases dens. We played kick-the-can; run, sheep, run; hide-the-thimble; and I-spy—games that never grow old. Our parents often played with us.

There were no games on Sundays though. On Saturday nights we shined our shoes, and on Sunday morning we dressed up in our best clothes to attend church and Sunday school. Usually we visited our granny in the afternoon; one granny one week and the other the next. Sunday evenings were a time to visit friends and neighbors. Often several families would gather for a hymn sing. My uncle used to give us a penny if we'd sing a song for him.

In school we learned the three R's, history, and geography. We did all our work on slates. We also memorized a great many Scriptures. These verses have been an inspiration to me all my life. We were taught obedience and respect for authority, and were expected to mind our manners. Every little girl was taught to sew, embroider, and knit at school, if she had not already learned these arts at home. The first thing we knitted was a scarf, of course. We used to stretch our scarfs to make them look longer. We were allowed to take them home, and our

[11]chuckies: jacks
[12]peery: a top

teacher didn't mind if the mothers helped by doing a few inches. But the next day she would hold up some poor child's scarf and say, "Aha! I see your mother did from here to here." We wondered how she knew.

Of course, when I was young, the heather did not bloom every day in Scotland, and I'm sure my parents were concerned about the coal supply, about providing warm clothing for a growing family, and about keeping our stomachs full in those uncertain years, but their faith in God sustained them. For us children it was a time of security, happy family relationships, and grateful acceptance of the daily blessings that were ours.

15

The Security of the Righteous

He that dwelleth in the secret place of the most High
Shall abide under the shadow of the Almighty.

I will say of the LORD,
He is my refuge and my fortress:
My God; in him will I trust.

Surely he shall deliver thee from the snare of the
      fowler,
And from the noisome pestilence.
He shall cover thee with his feathers,
And under his wings shalt thou trust:
His truth shall be thy shield and buckler.

Thou shalt not be afraid for the terror by night;
Nor for the arrow that flieth by day;
Nor for the pestilence that walketh in darkness;
Nor for the destruction that wasteth at noonday.

A thousand shall fall at thy side,
And ten thousand at thy right hand;
But it shall not come nigh thee.
Only with thine eyes shalt thou behold
And see the reward of the wicked.

Because thou hast made the LORD, which is my refuge,
Even the most High, thy habitation;
There shall no evil befall thee,
Neither shall any plague come nigh thy dwelling.

For he shall give his angels charge over thee,
To keep thee in all thy ways.
They shall bear thee up in their hands,
Lest thou dash thy foot against a stone.
Thou shalt tread upon the lion and adder:
The young lion and the dragon shalt thou trample under
feet.

Because he hath set his love upon me,
Therefore will I deliver him:
I will set him on high,
Because he hath known my name.

He shall call upon me, and I will answer him:
I will be with him in trouble;
I will deliver him, and honour him,
With long life will I satisfy him,
And shew him my salvation.

PSALM 91

16

 Danger in the Wind

BY ALAN S. PRIEST

It was such a peaceful, tranquil day that no one in the little Oregon school guessed the fearful excitement that was to come. Rays of bright May sunshine poured in on the students' desks. Fresh smells of spring drifted in the open windows. A hummingbird hovering outside one window seemed to say, "See what glorious things God has made!"

Twelve-year-old Stewart squirmed restlessly in his chair. Distracted by the hummingbird, he turned to look out the window. Oh, how nice it looked outside! Swallows were darting about. Green grass was beginning to appear, and water sparkled in the small creek that bordered the schoolyard. Beyond the creek, neighbor Anderson was plowing. "Sure wish I was on that tractor instead of in this schoolroom," Stewart thought to himself.

"Boys! Mind your lessons, please!" Brother Jonathan's clear voice rang across the room.

Startled, Stewart hastily turned to his workbook again. A quick movement on his left told him that his

younger brother Charles had also been caught day-
dreaming. Stewart noticed, though, that Charles was
frowning at the teacher. "Well," thought Stewart, "we
certainly can't blame Brother Jonathan. After all, he has
to stay in the classroom too. If only a breeze would come
up, it wouldn't be so warm in here."

Just then Brother Jonathan addressed his students
again. "I have decided this would be a good day to clean
up the schoolyard." He paused to run his fingers through
his curly black hair, a smile on his face. "Do I have any
volunteers?"

"Oh, can it be?" thought Stewart. "This is grand!" All
the children lifted their hands at once, boys and girls alike.

"Well," remarked Brother Jonathan, "such coopera-
tion!"

Outside in the yard, the students were grouped and
given tasks. The small children were to pick up litter,
and the older girls were to supervise them and empty
wastebaskets. The two oldest boys, Stewart and Charles,
were to help their teacher burn the dead grass behind
the schoolhouse.

When the two brothers received their assignment,
they exchanged questioning glances. Their teacher was
new to the area and did not realize the danger of burning on such a hot day. Stewart was about to say something when Brother Jonathan turned to him.

"Stewart," the teacher said, "there are some burlap
sacks in the woodshed. Both you and Charles take two
and go wet them in the creek. We do not have any shov-
els, but the air is so still that we shouldn't need any."

Before long, the boys stood by with the dripping
sacks in their hands, satisfied that their teacher's safety
measure would reduce the chance of a wildfire. Brother
Jonathan knelt and applied a match to the dry grass.
"Now, if the fire begins to burn where we don't want it to,

you boys beat it out with your wet sacks. That way we can control it."

For the first few minutes, all went according to plan. The boys walked slowly back and forth, beating occasionally at the edge of the fire while Brother Jonathan watched closely.

Then it happened! The breeze that Stewart had wished for earlier came, very suddenly. The fire responded with a leap. The gentle, smoldering blaze was suddenly a lunging enemy!

The boys jumped back with cries of alarm as sparks scorched them. Brother Jonathan's face was drawn with anxiety. "Girls!" he called anxiously. "You will have to help us! Wet more sacks in the creek and help beat the fire. Quickly!"

The fire was moving across the clearing toward the trees. Desperately the children and their teacher raced back and forth, beating at the fire with their sacks, trying to halt its progress.

They were getting nowhere. The wind was rising, carrying sparks ahead, starting more fires. It seemed that the small group was powerless to stop the flames.

One of the girls cried out, "The fire is among the trees!"

"Oh, no!" thought Stewart. "What will we do?" He prayed earnestly in his heart, "O dear God, please show us what to do. Please help us stop this fire."

Instantly a thought came to Stewart's mind. "Our school lane! It runs through the trees just up ahead."

Stepping back from the scorching edge of the fire, Stewart summoned the others excitedly. "If we run up the lane, we will be able to get ahead of the fire."

Brother Jonathan wiped the sweat on his face. "It could be dangerous, but it's our only chance!" he agreed. "The older girls must stay behind with the younger grades, though."

After wetting their sacks in the creek, the desperate trio raced ahead to cut off the fire. Its first point had just reached the lane; the graveled surface was already slowing its spread. With all the effort they could muster, Stewart, Charles, and Brother Jonathan attacked the flames. "We're gaining!" shouted Charles.

By running up and down the lane and beating out the leading edge of the fire, they finally brought the runaway under control. Brother Jonathan called to the older girls to bring water in the wastebaskets. Two hours and repeated trips for water followed; and finally the last flames were extinguished.

A very weary teacher led a group of very weary students back to the schoolhouse. The younger ones, however, were still not too tired to chatter excitedly about all that had taken place.

As they approached the building, they were met by neighbor Anderson, who roared up on his tractor, an anxious expression on his face. "I saw smoke over here and thought I should investigate," he said. "What happ—" His voice stopped in midsentence as he stared in wonder at the smudged, dirty, and rumpled appearance of the teacher and children.

Slowly Brother Jonathan gave an account of what had occurred.

Mr. Anderson shook his head. "That could have started a forest fire. I'm surprised that you were able to stop it."

"Well," answered Brother Jonathan soberly, "the fault for starting it is mine, but Stewart gets the credit for stopping it. He thought of catching it at the lane."

"No," Stewart said with a tired smile, "the credit goes to God; He gave me the idea. And after this, I'll be glad to sit in school, even on hot days, and I won't be wishing for any more excitement!"

17

 Outdoor Good Manners

AUTHOR UNKNOWN

Did you ever go into the woods to spend a few happy hours, only to find your favorite spot strewn with the remains of someone's picnic and perhaps a campfire still smoldering? If you have been disappointed by such a sight, no doubt you are resolved to be more thoughtful and considerate yourself in relation to "outdoor good manners."

The agencies that provide parks and tourist camps for the public must often be disappointed to see the way some people use them. In former days, when there were no automobiles, there were few parks or camps. They were not needed then, but with the world on wheels as it is today, thousands of parks are used.

Some people who have the best of manners at home seem to shed them as soon as they enter public grounds. When they have finished eating at home, they would not think of throwing the dishes in a corner or of dumping banana skins, eggshells, and tin cans in the middle of the floor. They would not burn the tablecloth and walk out of the house, leaving it afire. Yet while many people

70

would not think of doing these things in their own homes, they think nothing of doing them out-of-doors. Each year thousands of dollars and many hours are spent cleaning up parks and campsites after picnickers leave them.

Food and rubbish left lying about not only look very untidy; they also draw flies and spread disease. In addition, they encourage black bears to frequent such public areas, which is not a beneficial circumstance for either bears or campers! In nearly every park, rubbish and garbage containers are found, to make it easy for people to remember their outdoor good manners. Often there are signs that say, "This is your park. Help keep it clean," or, "Have you done your share?"

Many of our public parks and campsites are situated in forested areas. In spite of all that we can do to protect our forests, every year there are a great number of fires caused by careless individuals. These fires destroy countless numbers of beautiful trees, which makes all of us poorer. For although it takes only a few minutes for a tree to burn, it takes years and years for a forest to grow.

Before anyone leaves a campfire, he should be absolutely certain it is out. The most innocent-looking bed of ashes may have glowing coals underneath the surface. The ashes may be scattered by a sudden breeze and the live coals fanned into a blaze. The blaze may start a forest fire that may not only destroy property but also take human lives. An ounce of prevention in putting out a campfire may save a great deal of loss and suffering.

Many fires are caused by unthinking people throwing lighted cigars and cigarettes from their cars as they are riding along roads through our forests. This too is a negligent and dangerous display of outdoor bad manners.

Another outdoor bad habit is picking plants and flowers that grow in the parks. It is hard to give up picking these flowers, for we enjoy them so much that we wish to carry them back with us. But if we pick them, the individuals who come after us cannot have the same enjoyment we experienced.

Very few of us would think of going into a friend's garden and snatching his flowers when he was not looking. Yet that is no different from picking flowers in parks or public places. They are there for everyone to enjoy, not just for our own selfish pleasure. Some of the lovely blossoming things are not even picked carefully but are jerked up by the roots, so that the whole plant is destroyed.

Nature and the out-of-doors are a priceless gift that we should cherish and enjoy. One way we can do this is to show that we understand and appreciate the need for taking care of parks and campsites. Good manners should not be put on and off; they are for every day, indoors as well as outdoors.

18

The Crop of Acorns

There came a man in days of old
To hire a piece of land for gold,
And urged his suit in accents meek:
"One crop alone is all I seek;
The harvest o'er, my claim I'll yield
And to its lord return the field."

The owner some misgivings felt,
And coldly with the stranger dealt;
But found his last objection fail,
And honeyed argument prevail;
So took the offered price in hand,
And for "one crop" leased out the land.

The wily tenant sneered with pride,
And sowed the spot with acorns wide;
At first like tiny shoots they grew,
Then broad and wide their branches threw;
But long before those oaks could climb,
And finally reach their forest prime,
The cheated landlord moldering lay,
Forgotten, with his kindred clay.

O ye whose years, unfolding fair,
Are fresh with youth and free from care,
Should vice or laziness desire
The garden of your souls to hire,
No bargains make—reject the suit;
Don't let one seed the soil pollute.

My child, the first approach beware;
With firmness break the evil snare,
Lest, as the acorns grew and throve
Into a sun-excluding grove,
Thy sins, a dark o'ershadowing tree,
Shut out the light of heaven from thee.

L. H. SIGOURNEY

19

A Night on the Mississippi

AUTHOR UNKNOWN

I was nearly fourteen years old when I made my first trip down the Mississippi River. Father had a good crop of early spring vegetables, and my elder brother James and I were eager to carry them to market. Father owned a large raft, which he and James had made, and we were sure that we could take care of ourselves and the produce too.

So at last Father gave his consent. He built a cabin near one end of the raft, where we could stay when it rained or when the sun was too hot. The floor of the cabin was six or seven inches above the deck of the raft, and here we could keep our clothes and blankets and the food for our journey. At one side of the cabin we made a layer of dirt about five or six inches deep with a frame around it to hold it in place. Then with some bricks and clay we built a small fireplace. Here we could have a fire if the weather became wet or chilly.

James made some extra steering oars, for it was easy to break one if the raft went over a snag; and we rigged up a forked stick on which we hung our lantern. We had to carry a light, of course, or the steamboats on the river would have run us down.

The river was still high after the June rise, and the lowest banks were a little under water.

"There won't be much danger from the upstream boats," said Father when he came down to see us off. "They'll make for the smooth water alongshore. But keep your eyes and your ears open for the boats that are going your way. Good-bye, boys, and be careful!"

I stood up and waved to him as long as I could see him, but a curve in the river soon hid him from sight. The current was running more than four miles an hour and I was astonished to see how the familiar shores slipped away from us. In a big bend on the Illinois side was an island where we had often gone for picnics and hikes. The sandbar at its head was completely under water, and the tree trunks stood up out of the river, straight and black, as if they too were floating downstream on a voyage of discovery.

I am sure that Columbus sailing out into the trackless sea was not more convinced of the greatness of his task than I was as I took my turn at the steering oar to let James eat his dinner. The unwieldly raft yielded to my guidance, and for the mere fun of it I kept its course a winding one for the next half-hour.

The river was full of driftwood, and all sorts of strange things could be seen. A straw bed with an old tin coffeepot upon it came floating along beside us. Once a hungry rabbit ran across a broken tree trunk to the raft, and I gave him a handful of lettuce as I would have fed a pet lamb. As soon as he had eaten it, all his shyness came back to him and he raced off again to the farther end of his log, where he sat and watched us for a long time.

As the shadows grew longer, I began to feel drowsy.

The soft air fanned me gently, and the lap of the water against the timbers of the raft was very soothing. Before I knew it, I was fast asleep. When I woke, I had at first no idea where I was. The moon was shining, and the river looked as if it were miles wide. We were near the Illinois shore, in the quiet water under the bank; and across the gleaming sheet of silver, I could see high bluffs on the Missouri side.

I heard the sound of voices and saw that James was talking to a man in buckskins who had come aboard to share our supper and to tell us the news. The raft was made fast to a towhead—a sandbar covered with cottonwood trees—and the stranger's skiff lay alongside. On the black hillsides behind us I could see a few gleaming lights, but there was stillness everywhere except for an occasional *kerchug* from some wakeful bullfrog. We seemed to have the whole river to ourselves.

The trapper was telling stories of his life in the wilderness, and I listened with infinite wonder and delight. Occasionally we saw steamboats going up the river. Now and then one would send up a shower of sparks that rained down onto the river again and made the moonlight look pale. Then a bend of the stream would hide their lights, and after a long time their waves would reach us and rock the raft up and down in a most delightful fashion.

I was no longer sleepy, and the charm of a new experience kept me awake for the greater part of the night. The people on shore went to bed, the lights winked out, our new friend and James were presently sound asleep; but I lay and watched for the coming of the early dawn.

First, looking away over the water, I could see a dull, dark line; that was the wooded shore of the other side. The birds twittered softly in the trees close at hand. Finally there came a faint, pale light in the sky; then the river softened from black to gray; and far out I could see small, dusky spots drifting along.

Once there was a long, black line which I knew was a raft like ours, only much larger and heavier. I faintly heard the raftmen's voices and a steering oar creaking. Then a streak on the water showed where a snag lay hidden beneath, ready to catch and snap some unwary oar. By and by the mist drew itself up from the river in fleecy twists and swirls, and the east began to redden, a breeze sprang up, and lines of smoke rose from the hillside behind us. At last the full day broke, and everything smiled in the sunshine.

Far off another raft glided by. A man on it was chopping wood. I lay on a pile of blankets, my head pillowed on my arm, watching the ax flash and come down. An instant later it would be lifted for another stroke—still no sound—and then, as the ax was poised above the man's head, the ring of the first stroke would reach my listening ears. As I watched, my eyelids grew heavier and heavier.

"Come, come, lad!" said James, shaking me good-humoredly. "The bacon is ready to eat, and it's time we were moving. We shall never get there if you are going to sleep all day."

I sat up with a start and rubbed my eyes. The trapper's skiff was gone, the sun was high in the heavens, and the fried bacon sent forth a savory invitation to breakfast. My first night on the Mississippi was over.

20

 Looking at the Other Side

BY MARÍA JUANA DE MEJÍA

Part I

"Grown-ups!" Armando[1] said with a scowl as he crouched in the tall grass. "They're all alike. Always against me!" From his hiding place, Armando could see Brother Montealegre,[2] his teacher, on the schoolhouse porch, anxiously looking for him. "I wonder if he thinks I'm going to go back into that classroom."

Only fifteen minutes earlier, Armando had been at his desk—a part of the Valle Lindo School of twenty pupils. But he had not been studying. Instead, he had been stealthily counting a small pile of coins and a few bills. "Five colons and seventy-five centavos," he murmured happily to himself. "Maybe I have enough to buy a sweet as well as my pocketknife."

Ever since he could remember, Armando had wanted a pocketknife, a knife that would really cut. There were so many things a boy could do with a knife. And now, at last, he had earned enough money to buy one.

[1]Armando (är män´ dō)
[2]Montealegre (môn tä ä lĕg´ rä)

79

Just as Armando began to dream of the wooden figures he would carve and of the times he would hit the
target on tree trunks with his knife, he felt a hand on his
shoulder. Startled, he looked up to meet the dark eyes of
Brother Montealegre.

"Have you finished your mathematics?" the teacher
asked. Then holding out his hand, he added, "I'll take
care of your money until recess time."

Reluctantly Armando placed all his precious money
in the outstretched hand. As Armando bent back to his
work, he thought resentfully, "The teacher has no right
to take my money."

Back at his desk, Brother Montealegre counted the
money before putting it away. "Five seventy-five," he
said to himself thoughtfully. "That's strange. I don't
want to believe that Armando has returned to his habit
of 'picking up' money here and there. But only yesterday
Rodrigo came to me upset because a little more than this
amount had disappeared from his jacket pocket. I'll have
to check into this later," he decided as he turned back to
his pupils.

At recess time, Brother Montealegre called Armando
to him. "Armando," he began, "you realize, don't you,
that you are not to be doing other things during study
time until your work is completed?"

"Yes," answered Armando with downcast eyes.

"Then be sure you apply yourself more diligently in
the future. You will not be punished this time." Then as
he handed back the bills and coins, Brother Montealegre
inquired, "May I ask, by the way, how you came to have
so much money?"

"I earned it chopping weeds after school," Armando
replied grudgingly.

"Did you know Rodrigo missed almost this very
amount yesterday?"

"But that has nothing to do with me," asserted Armando. "I'm sure I don't know what happened to his money."

"I'll go call Rodrigo," said his teacher. "You wait here, please."

Armando was puzzled. Did the teacher think he had *taken* Rodrigo's money? Why, it had been all of a month or two since he had picked up anything that was not his. Then a truly frightening thought came to him. What if Rodrigo should claim to recognize a particular coin he had? What if he could not make them believe him? They must not take his money away from him. He had almost felt that pocketknife in his hand, and now he could not bear to lose it.

Armando thought rapidly. Neither Brother Montealegre nor Rodrigo was yet in sight. Desperately, Armando bolted for the door. Once outside, he ran swiftly across the schoolyard toward a cover of bushes and trees. Just as he reached the edge of the cover, he heard a classmate shout, "Armando's running away!"

He kept running, then threw himself face down in an area of dense brush. He was sure the teacher would not find him there even if he did leave classwork to search for him—an unlikely possibility.

Armando had ridden a horse to school that morning. Now he thought. "If only I could get to my horse, I could get away faster." But he had left the horse tied to the fence on the other side of the building. Did he dare risk being seen? Moving slowly and always keeping low, he crept into the high pasture bordering the schoolhouse. Once he raised his head cautiously to peer at the building and saw Brother Montealegre on the porch, scanning the area carefully. He could hear him calling his name. It was then that Armando began to mutter his feelings against adults.

The boy had never known his parents. He had never fallen asleep in his mother's arms. He had never clambered onto his father's lap or known what it was like to have brothers or sisters to play with.

Armando had been a street urchin with no home but the thoroughfares of San Salvador. The earliest bed he could remember was a piece of cardboard laid in a shop doorway. His meals were snatched at odd moments from garbage cans, and his pastime was filching fruits from street vendors or coins from newspaper boys. His friends were homeless and uncared-for like himself—all compelled to fight for their living.

Out of this way of life had risen Armando's distrust of adults. He could recall a time when a truck driver had offered, "You may sleep on top of my load of sugar cane tonight." The driver had not mentioned that he planned to drive farther that night. Armando had climbed up and gratefully settled to sleep, glad that for once he had a place softer than the cold sidewalk. Even now he could remember his bewilderment and terror when he awoke to find the truck rolling and pitching down the highway. At last it had stopped in a distant city. The truck driver had merely laughed at the frightened, frustrated boy—a joke, he had called it.

Worst of all had been the civil guards. Time and time again when Armando and some friends were playing on the street at dusk, they would be approached by one or more uniformed men. "Come," they would call. "Come with us; we'll find you a place to sleep."

The first time, Armando had been thankful to go with them. But he soon learned that their "place to sleep" was a section of the jail. There he had to spend the night with several dozen other street children. He knew that the guards said it was for their own protection against real criminals of the night and that they would be released in the morning. Nevertheless, Armando grew to hate this treatment at the hand of grown-ups. He became suspicious in nature and unwilling to trust anyone much older than himself.

When Armando was ten, a Christian farmer named Franco Muñoz had chatted with him on the street. Franco was impressed by Armando's resolute spirit and felt compassion for the homeless boy. After talking it over with his wife, Mayra, they had decided to care for Armando—perhaps he could take the place of the son they had never had. The Muñoz family was poor, but at least Armando now had a place to call home for as long as he chose.

At first he was wary of the Muñozes—was this another grown-up trap? But as the couple continued to treat him kindly, he began slowly to believe that there might be grown-ups after all who were not bent on deceiving youngsters.

For the most part, Armando was happy in his new life; living in the country was an adventure for him. Yet there were times when a life of schedule—regular meals, work at certain hours, school every day—seemed overwhelmingly restrictive. He felt choked by the routine and penned in by the lack of his former freedom. In spite of all the advantages of his new life—food, a real bed, the chance to attend school—he more than once felt a great urge to run back to the streets.

But he had never actually run away—until now. Brother Montealegre had seemed to be the kind of person he might be able to trust. But, no; now Armando felt he was no different from the others.

And so he crouched in the grass, watching for a chance to get to his horse. Finally the teacher gave up his search and entered the building. Armando edged closer and rose cautiously out of the grass. No one was in sight.

Now was his chance. He would leap onto his horse and be off at a gallop—away from the teacher and his unspoken accusation—away from the stifling routine of school.

His horse! It was not in its place! Dismayed, he cast a worried look around and saw it tied to a post right up by the schoolhouse door. Once again someone had gotten the best of him; once again someone was working against him. At that moment Brother Montealegre reappeared on the porch. This time Armando could not duck in time and the teacher, spying him, called, "Armando, come. I want to talk with you."

His voice sounded kind enough, but suddenly all the wrongs of all the adults in his past life welled up inside Armando in a furious rage. He would not be fooled again by any adult. "I'm not coming!" he shouted to Brother Montealegre.

"Come, let's talk," urged his teacher. "I won't punish you for running away. Let's just talk."

"No!" shouted Armando. "I know you. You say you won't do anything to me, but when I get there you'll punish me. It's all a trick!"

"Please, please believe me," pleaded the man again.

Armando's own shouting had emboldened him. Now, nearly crying in his fury, he yelled, "No, I'm never coming back! I know you're not really my friend. I'll *never* obey you anymore!"

And with that he bolted once more for the thicket. He *had* to get away from this world controlled by deceiving adults.

Brother Montealegre, grieved by the boy's action, returned to his desk. His troubled gaze rested on Armando's empty chair. He sighed deeply. "I've tried to show Armando that I love him. Where have I failed? How can I prove I'm not against him? When will he believe me?"

"Please, God," he prayed. "Show me what I can do."

PART II

Meanwhile, Armando returned to his hiding place in the thicket and threw himself on the ground. He hardly knew what to do. "I'll wait," he muttered at last, "until I'm sure he's gone; then I'll get my horse. And no one will stop me!"

The hours passed slowly. It grew cooler and a steady rain began to fall. Armando shivered as a brisk wind cut through the brush around him. It was dark before he finally stole cautiously across the schoolyard and untied his horse.

Once mounted, he became unsure of himself. "Where shall I go now?" It was night and he was not in the big city of San Salvador, where a person could always scrounge something to eat. This was a countryside of poor farmers. The city lay hours away. Much as he hated to face his guardians, the Muñozes, he realized that going to their house was the only chance he had of finding food and shelter that night.

It was a hard decision. Pulled by a desire for more freedom, yet constrained by the kindness and care that Franco and Mayra had shown him, Armando at last made his choice and turned his horse in the direction of the Muñoz farm. "I suppose the teacher has already been there and told them about me," he muttered half angrily. "But no one will listen to *my* side of the story. Which of the grown-ups is going to believe me? They will band together against me."

When at last a much-troubled Armando turned into the Muñoz yard, bone-weary and bedraggled, he expected nothing but harsh words and a severe punishment. How surprised he was to see Mayra fling the door open and to hear her say, "You poor fellow! Come in right away." She bustled about, preparing hot tea and saying, "You must take a bath and put on dry clothes while I fix you a bite to eat."

Before long, Armando was eating hungrily of the bread and cheese set before him. He dared not ask why he was not being punished. He was still eating when Franco entered. "You're back, thank God," the man said quietly with a happy glow in his face.

"Yes," acknowledged the boy sullenly. "But," he declared, "I'm never going back to that school again."

"We'll talk about that later," Franco told him. "The best thing for you now is a bed."

As tired as he was, Armando offered no objections and headed for bed. But he was greatly puzzled. "What's this?" he wondered. "Aren't they going to punish me?"

The next morning after coffee, Franco called Armando aside. "I'd like to talk to you a bit before school," he began.

"But I'm not going," interrupted Armando.

Overlooking this, Franco said, "Yesterday afternoon Brother Montealegre came and talked with us. He was disappointed and sad because of a misunderstanding he had with you over some money."

"Sad!" retorted Armando. "He's only trying to trap me to take my money away from me."

"Armando, let me see one of your coins," requested Franco.

Reluctantly Armando pulled a five-centavo piece from his pocket and handed it to Franco, wondering what was coming next.

Franco took the coin between two fingers, and holding it out toward Armando he asked, "Armando, tell me what you see on this coin."

Still wondering what Franco was doing, Armando said slowly, "I see the figure of a man's head."

"Anything else?"

"Well, around the edge of the coin are the words 'Republic of El Salvador.' At the bottom is the year when the coin was made."

"Fine," said Franco. "Now I will tell you what I see when I look at this coin. I see a big numeral '5' with the word 'centavos' below it. Encircling this is a wreath of leaves and berries."

"Armando," he asked, "are both of us looking at the same coin?"

"Of course," answered the boy.

"Then why do you see one design when you look at it, and I see a completely different design?"

Armando told him readily, "That's because you're looking at one side of it and I'm looking at the other side. But it's the same coin." In his concentration on the coin, he momentarily forgot his problem with his teacher.

"Well said!" answered Franco, pleased. "Now, Armando, do you know that most problems are like this coin?"

"What do you mean?" asked Armando.

"Often when there is a misunderstanding between two persons, there is more than one side to the misunderstanding. Do you know what I am saying?"

"I suppose there can be two sides," replied Armando.

"Right. You know, what makes a misunderstanding really sad is when neither of the two persons takes time to see the problem from the other's side. Many problems can be solved if we learn to look at more than our own side. Now let's think about Brother Montealegre and you. How do you feel about the problem?"

"It makes me angry that the teacher accused me of stealing. I think he wants to take my money, and he mustn't. I worked for it."

"And how do you think this matter looks from Brother Montealegre's side?"

"I don't know," answered Armando, not sure it was worth considering.

"Armando, do you think the teacher had any reason to think you might have taken Rodrigo's money?" Not waiting for an answer, Franco continued, "Some months ago, money was missing from the teacher's cash box. Who had taken it?"

Without saying a word, Armando hung his head.

"Then a few weeks later, some coins were missing from Saedy's desk. Again, who was guilty? Is it so strange that the teacher should question you about Rodrigo's money?"

Was Franco saying it was his own fault that Brother Montealegre had questioned him? Armando did not want to believe it, yet seen from this new side, it did look as if the teacher had reason to suspect that he may have stolen the money.

"Now let's think about something else. You became angry and disappointed that the teacher should suspect you. Think about the things you shouted to him. Of course, you know you were not being respectful. But even apart from that, how do you think this business made him feel?"

"I don't know."

"I do know. He told me. He said he did not want to believe you had turned to picking up money again. He wanted to assure himself that it had *not* been you; that was why he wanted to check into the matter carefully. He is disappointed, too—disappointed that a pupil he loves could have such bitter feelings toward him. He feels very sad about it. Grown-ups can hurt inside as well as youngsters, Armando."

This was something the boy had never thought about. The idea that not all grown-ups were hardhearted remained difficult for the boy to accept.

"Now, Armando, think carefully. Has the teacher ever really tricked you? Has he ever been insincere with you? Has he treated you unkindly? Have you ever had a reason before this to think he treated you unfairly?"

Armando was silent for a long moment, thinking back over the period he had known Brother Montealegre. Truly, he could not recall a single incident in which his teacher had not tried to be fair.

At last Franco asked quietly, "Do you think maybe *you* were accusing *him* falsely?"

As Armando thought about his own behavior, he began to feel a deep shame. Could it be that the teacher really had not been trying to fool him at all? Could it be that everything would have worked out well if he had stayed in the classroom instead of running away? Had he perhaps made matters worse by seeing the issue only from his own side? He considered the coin Franco had handed back to him. Yes, it certainly did look different depending which side one looked at.

"Armando," said Franco. "Let's pray about it now. Then I'm going to let you decide which day you'll go back to school and what you should say to Brother Montealegre."

Then Franco prayed, "God, both the teacher and Armando are hurting inside. Show Armando what he can do to make things right. Help him to be honest always and to learn to see problems from both sides. In Jesus' Name, amen."

When Armando walked back into the classroom the next morning, no one was quicker to greet him or had a bigger smile for him than Brother Montealegre. Going to him, he laid a hand on his shoulder. "Armando," he said. "I'm so glad to see you back. I'm sorry I did not give you a chance to explain how you came by the money. Forgive me, please."

"And I'm sorry I ran away and said such nasty things to you, Brother Montealegre," answered Armando shamefacedly. "Now I believe that not all grown-ups are working against me." Hesitantly, he thrust a small package into the teacher's hand. "For you," he said simply and turned to go to his desk.

Brother Montealegre opened it to find a lovely pen. Armando glanced up from his seat and was surprised to see the teacher's eyes fill with tears as he read the accompanying note, "To my fine teacher. With love, Armando."

Only the Muñozes, Armando, and God knew that Armando's own precious money had bought this gift. But somehow Armando felt he had used his hard-earned two-sided coins for something of greater worth than a pocketknife.

21

Growing Smiles

A smile is quite a funny thing—
    It wrinkles up your face,
And when it's gone, you never find
    Its secret hiding place.

But far more wonderful it is
    To see what smiles can do;
You smile at one, he smiles at you,
    And so one smile makes two.

He smiles at someone since you smiled,
    And then that one smiles back;
And that one smiles, until in truth
    You fail in keeping track.

Now since a smile can do great good
    By cheering hearts of care,
Let's smile and smile, and not forget
    That smiles go everywhere.

AUTHOR UNKNOWN

22

Flat-tail:
An Autumn Night
in the Life of a Beaver

BY ALAN S. PRIEST

"And the Spirit of God moved upon the face of the waters" (Genesis 1:2). So it seemed, for the water in the beaver pond was very still and all was silent. The twilight held an air of mystery, and there was a sharp sense of autumn chill in the air. Only the sporadic knocking of a woodpecker on a dead tree broke the stillness.

Suddenly the smooth surface of the pond was divided by a V-shaped ripple. At the leading point of the ripple was a brown body with head and square-cornered nose held high. It was Flat-tail the beaver, checking the air for any scent of intruders. He was an old beaver, twelve years of age and weighing almost sixty pounds. His flat tail was slashed and scarred from numerous battles fought with other beavers.

Satisfied that all was safe in the vicinity of his pond, Flat-tail set about his first task of the evening: checking the condition of the main dam.

A short distance behind him, another brown head

surfaced. This was his mate. The two swam rapidly toward the dam, their large webbed hind feet pushing them and their flat tails serving as rudders.

On reaching the dam, they chased away an old mink that had taken up residence there. Unperturbed, he would return when their work was finished. He had long since accepted their evening arrival as an unavoidable inconvenience.

The dam spanned a small creek, thus creating the pond. It was constructed of alternate layers of sticks and branches, old logs, and mud, and was almost eighty yards long. Some parts of it were four feet high, and its base was about five feet wide. Not straight, the dam was made stronger by the curving line it followed across the head of the pond.

Near the center of the dam, the beavers had constructed a trail leading to an adjoining pond below. This trail was really more of a slide. Formed in the earth of the dam, it was kept slick by the wet bodies of the beavers as they slid from one pond to the next. Besides the beaver family and the old mink, muskrats and an occasional otter were known to use this trail.

Below the main pond were five more dams. Each was on a lower level, and each backed up a small pond of its own. The smaller dams served to relieve the pressure on the main dam. Each smaller dam also had a slide-trail over it, which gave the beavers convenient access to all the ponds. For water animals, the beaver pond was a city-center, complete with overpasses!

As Flat-tail began inspecting the main dam, his mate went down the slide to check the lower dams. Soon Flat-tail found a low spot that did not suit him, and his evening labor began. Diving underwater, he came up with a quantity of mud from the bottom. He carried it by holding it against his chest with his two front feet. Then he dropped it where it was needed and used his front feet to pat it down. Flat-tail repeated this procedure several times before he was satisfied.

With his inspection of the main dam complete, Flat-tail started for the felling area. God has placed in beavers the instinct to know that when autumn arrives, they must store up enough food to last through the winter. Flat-tail's family would require the bark and twigs from about one acre of poplars and willows over the next year.

At this pond, the beavers had cleared all the green poplars for a distance of about a hundred yards back from the water's edge. For two-thirds of this distance, the beavers had dug a canal about two feet wide and two feet deep. This was for safety. Slow and cumbersome on land, Flat-tail was no match for lynx, wolverines, and timber wolves—his natural enemies. But once in the water, he could easily outstrip these predators.

Coming to the end of the canal, Flat-tail began traveling the remaining thirty-five yards on foot. The trail he followed was worn straight and smooth by the numerous trees that had been dragged over it. At the felling area,

the ground was covered by a jumble of fallen trees and debris. A beaver is not able to direct which way a tree will fall; so some trees, cut through at the stump, were leaning into others while some lay about in a jumble of trunks and branches.

Beavers are equipped with four long teeth in the front of their mouths, two in the upper jaw and two in the lower. Turning his head sideways, Flat-tail set to work on a small poplar. He first made two cuts about two inches apart, and then he tore out the wood in between. By repeating this procedure, he had the five-inch tree severed in about ten minutes. Cutting wood is something beavers must do, for their front teeth never stop growing and must constantly be worn down by chewing.

After felling several more trees, Flat-tail returned to the pond. Night had fallen, and it was time to recruit help.

On arriving at his lodge in the middle of the pond, Flat-tail dived and entered through one of the underwater doorways. The lodge, like the dam, was made of mud and sticks. It measured twenty-five feet in diameter at the base and extended from the pond bottom to about six feet above its surface. It had several underwater entrances, though the living quarters were in the part that rose above the water. Warm and dry inside the lodge was Flat-tail's family of kits (born in the spring) and yearling beavers (born in the previous spring). Flat-tail communicated to the yearling beavers that they were to help bring in the branches which would provide the family's winter food. The kits would stay behind.

Leaving the lodge, Flat-tail surfaced about thirty feet away and soon found his mate, who had returned from her tour of inspection. Nothing was amiss in the lower ponds, so the parents and a trail of younger beavers set a course for the felling area.

There followed several hours of industrious activity.

The beavers hurried up and down the thirty-five-yard trail, carrying and dragging branches to the canal. The two older beavers brought heavier pieces and the younger beavers brought lighter ones. They communicated by squealing and grunting in their beaver language as they worked.

Coming to the pond with their burdens, the beavers floated them toward the lodge, directing the pieces by pushing with their noses. They hooked some pieces under the edge of the lodge and pushed the ends of some into the soft, muddy bottom near a lodge entrance. Other pieces they wove or meshed in with the ones already there. In this way the beaver family stored their winter supply of food underwater so that it would be beneath the winter ice.

Things were going well until, on a return trip for more trees, Flat-tail's keen ears detected the sound of an intruder. What could it be? Was it the lynx that had killed two of his children in the spring? Flat-tail sounded the alarm—he lifted his large, flat tail and struck the water with a resounding *smack!* The report was like a rifle shot. Hearing it, the landlocked beavers lumbered down the slope and into the canal as fast as they were able. They ran at an awkward gallop, with their tails held straight out, off the ground. Even after his family was safe in the lodge, Flat-tail continued to swim back and forth, striking the water several more times with his tail. Perhaps he was mocking old Mister Lynx.

By now it was time to halt the night's activities anyway, for the sun would soon be up. Flat-tail's family would stay in the lodge the remainder of the night to rest and eat; then they would sleep through the daylight hours. For now, Flat-tail would simply float in the water for a little while and enjoy the early morning stillness. After all, the pond would soon freeze over, and then he would not be able to do this for a long time.

23

A Simple Kind of Bravery

BY ELIZABETH WAGLER

Part I

Esther trailed slowly behind the herd of Holstein cows as they ambled toward the barn and the evening milking. Her eyes we fixed on her rubber boots as they swished through the sparse grass; her mind was far away.

She imagined herself standing beside a deep, fast-flowing stream. Suddenly she sees a small child on the opposite back slip and fall into the water. Instantly, Esther dives into the stream; the current catches her, and it is all she can do to reach the child. With her strength almost gone, she starts toward the bank . . .

Woof! Woof! Woof! Esther was jerked sharply from her reverie as Blondie, her yellow collie, hurtled past her, barking furiously. She looked up quickly and sighed, "Oh, there goes Ethel again." Ethel was the most ornery cow. She always waited until the herd was almost at the barn before breaking away and tearing off to the far corner of the field. As Esther broke into a run, she reminded herself ruefully that if she had been paying attention,

97

she would not be chasing Ethel around the field now.

Later that evening, after the dishes were done, Esther and her younger sisters, Mary and Eva, were playing with the kittens in the front lawn. Esther was still dreaming about being brave. Her favorite heroine was Esther in the Bible, who courageously did her part to save her nation from death. How Esther longed to be brave and fearless like Esther in the Bible! Unfortunately, she didn't think she was brave at all.

As Esther watched Mary and Eva teasing the kittens with pieces of string, her eyes wandered to the upstairs balcony. "I wonder," she mused, "if I'd be brave enough the get onto the house roof? It doesn't look like it would be too scary."

"Hey, girls," she called. "Do you think I would be brave enough to climb onto the roof?"

Mary and Eva raised round eyes up, up, to the roof line.

"O-o-oh, you couldn't do that," Mary breathed in awe.

"I'm going to try," Esther asserted, springing to her feet.

She ran into the house, and in a few minutes she appeared on the upstairs balcony. While her audience watched admiringly, she crawled along the outside edge of the balcony until she could drop onto the lower roof of the summer kitchen.

"Now I'm going to get up onto the house roof," she called down. She did not notice that Eva had disappeared.

"Esther," Mother's stern vice floated up from the lawn. "You come down this minute!"

Shamefacedly, Esther retraced her adventurous steps.

"What were you doing on the roof?" demanded Mother when Esther at last had her feet firmly on the ground.

"She was being brave," piped up Mary loyally.

"Brave?" Mother looked from Mary to Esther with a puzzled frown. She studied her oldest daughter curiously. "Does that explain why you were trying to ride the calves in the orchard the other evening?"

Esther nodded unhappily. "I'd like to be brave like Esther in the Bible," she admitted. "But I'm not," she finished miserably.

"Walking around on the roof and riding half-wild calves is not being brave," Mother declared. "That is being foolish. You are brave enough for a twelve-year-old girl," she encouraged.

Esther looked up. "How am I brave?"

"Well," Mother pointed out, "you watch the baby for an hour every night while I go to the barn for milking."

"That isn't being brave," objected Esther. "That is fun."

"Some twelve-year-olds wouldn't want to stay alone in the house with their little brother," Mother replied. "And the other night when Blondie was missing, you went out and looked for her," reminded Mother.

"But I was scared stiff out there in the dark." Esther shuddered at the memory. "I didn't feel brave at all."

"Do you think Esther in the Bible felt brave when she stood before the king?"

"I don't know."

"I suspect that she was shaking from head to foot," Mother commented soberly. "She likely thought that within a few hours she would face a terrible death. She had no way of knowing that her name would go down in history for her courageous act. She simply did what had to be done and trusted God to give her the strength to do it.

"Brave deeds are not premeditated, nor are they done to impress others," Mother went on to explain. "As the eldest girl, you should be more concerned with setting a proper example for your sisters to follow than with trying to prove to them that you are brave." With that, Mother patted Esther on the shoulder and turned to go back to the house.

Esther felt ashamed. She was glad Mother had reproved her, and she decided that she would stop worrying about being brave and instead try to do as her mother advised. She could hear Mary and Eva playing around the corner of the house, and with a smile she ran off to join them.

PART II

Esther rolled over sleepily and glanced at her alarm clock. Six-thirty. Too early to get up yet. In the dim light she saw that Mother had laid out their Sunday dresses and stockings. She could hear her mother now, singing in the kitchen below as she prepared breakfast. From the direction of the barn came the faint *chug-chug-chug* of the milking machine. Her eyelids dropped. . . .

"Y-e-e-e-e-e-e!" A long, piercing shriek jerked her wide awake.

"Help! Fire! *Fire!*"

Esther leaped out of bed and flew to the window. Her grandmother was running across the lawn, yelling as she went, "Fire—the house is on fire!"

By the time Esther could open the window to hear better, Father, Grandpa, and the hired man were running toward the house, followed by an excited Grandma. "In the cellar," she was calling after them, "the furnace . . . house full of smoke . . . whole cellar in flames!"

Esther's grandparents lived in the *daudyhouse,*[1] an addition attached to the south end of their long farmhouse.

[1]daudyhouse (dô´ dē hous): addition to the main house (or small house located near the main house) that many Amish and Mennonite people build for their elderly parents

If the daudyhouse burned, the main house could burn too.

Esther was trembling. What should she do? What had she been told? "Get out," Father had said. "In case of fire, get out as soon as you can; and if there is no other way, then jump."

Esther glanced dubiously out the window to the concrete sidewalk two stories below. Well, she could not see flames anywhere. Such drastic action did not seem to be called for at this point. But the little children? She looked toward Mary and little Eva in the double bed across the room, and baby Paul in his crib. She should get them out of the burning house. Where could she take them? It was November. There was frost on the grass. They could not just stand in the yard in their bare feet and nightclothes.

She dashed from the room and tumbled down the steps. Her mother was standing by the phone, dialing. Esther tugged at her sleeve. "Shall I take the little children out to the car?" she whispered urgently.

Mother nodded gratefully and then spoke into the receiver. "Hello? Yes, we have a fire. . . ."

Esther ran up the stairs back to her room. She shook her little sisters awake. "The house is on fire," she explained briefly, snatching blankets and quilts from the beds. "Quick, get up and we'll go sit in the car until the firemen come."

Mary rubbed her eyes sleepily. "Where is the fire? I don't see any fire."

Eva began to whimper. "I want Mother."

Esther pushed a rolled-up quilt into the arms of each little girl and shoved them gently toward the hall. Then she turned to the crib where baby Paul was reaching out his arms to her, gurgling happily. "At least you are in a good mood," she said with a smile as she deftly folded blankets around him. Struggling with the squirming bundle in her arms, Esther herded her reluctant sisters down the stairs, through the now-empty kitchen, and onto the porch at the far end of the house. Between her and the car shed stretched over a hundred feet of frost-encrusted grass. Esther gritted her teeth, and clutching the baby tightly, she ran. The icy ground stung her bare feet. She deposited her burden on the back seat of the car and turned to see if Mary and Eva were coming. There they stood on the porch, shivering and crying loudly, their blanket bundles trailing forlornly behind them. It looked as though Esther would have to go back and get them.

Taking Eva on her back, she grasped Mary's hand and pleaded, "Come, I'll help you run." But Mary refused.

"It's too cold," she wailed. "I don't want to go to the car." Without further ado, Esther trotted to the shed with Eva on her back and returned to repeat the performance with Mary.

When all the three children were wrapped in quilts, she carefully started the car as Father had taught her, being careful to open the window a crack. With the heater running, they would soon be warm. The girls had stopped crying, so Esther took a few minutes to rub her own chilled feet. "I should have taken time to dress," she thought regretfully.

The baby began to whimper and struggle in his blankets.

"He's hungry," decided Esther. "Mary, you take care of Paul while I run and fetch a bottle."

"You'll get all burned up!" protested Mary as her older sister made her exit.

After looking to make sure that no one would see her in her nightclothes, Esther sped back over the cold grass.

By now, the smell of smoke was strong in the house, so she lost no time in preparing a bottle for the baby and finding a coat for herself. Once outside, she found that a large number of neighbors had arrived to help in the emergency.

The front door banged open behind Esther, and Father staggered out, carrying Mother's sewing cabinet. The foot control of the machine dragged behind and clattered on the porch steps.

Esther almost cried out, "Be careful! You're breaking it!" but Father called to the men on the lawn, "Could you start bringing things out of the house! And don't worry about damaging anything."

The men sprang into action, and Esther started back to her charges.

Back in the car, the baby contentedly sucked on his bottle while the three girls peered anxiously from the windows. They could see men rushing out of the house, carrying chairs, couches, the washing machine, drawers, and armfuls of clothing. Quilts and pillows were sailing from the upstairs windows and falling in soft heaps on the damp grass.

Soon plumes of smoke were billowing from the far end of the house. More and more neighbors were coming. Cars were lining up along the road. Esther wished she could see more of the daudyhouse from where she was, but it was hidden by a corner of the car shed.

Wh-e-e-e-o-o-o-h! Whe-e-e-o-o-o-h!

It was the fire trucks! Esther pulled Eva onto the seat so she could see better. Fire trucks! At their house! Mary and Eva jumped up and down in excitement. But the fun did not last long. The red engines continued toward the daudyhouse and disappeared from view.

The next two hours dragged for Esther. Right in her own yard, most of the neighborhood was gathered. Two shiny red fire engines pumped water. Black-clad firemen dragged fire hoses across the lawn, and flames shot from the windows—or so she imagined. And here she sat in the midst of all this excitement—in the car shed, in her nightclothes, missing everything.

She rocked the baby, sang songs to the girls, and kept them from getting out of the car to look for Mother. Several times Esther herself tried to leave, but the girls would not let her, and she knew she really should not leave them alone with the car running. So she stayed, doing her best to keep them happy.

Finally Uncle Russell walked into the shed. "I suppose you'd like to see what's going on?" he asked.

"Oh, yes!" cried Esther. "But we aren't dressed."

"I'll go see if your mother has time to find some clothes for you," Uncle Russell promised.

"Is our house all burned up now?" Eva wanted to know.

"No," he chuckled, "The firemen have the fire almost out. Grandpa's house is burned badly inside, but it didn't fall down, and your part of the house didn't even start burning."

"But why did they throw all our things outside?" wondered Mary.

"They thought the house might burn," explained Uncle Russell as he turned to leave.

Soon Mother came with their clothes. Her face was streaked with soot and her hair was all stringy. She hugged the baby and spoke over her shoulder to Esther. "Thank you, Esther, for taking care of the children. You did the right thing."

At last Esther was able to join the crowd around the daudyhouse. Many of the neighbors had already left. The firemen were rolling up the hoses. Esther could see through the open basement door that everything inside was black.

They did not go to church that Sunday. The cows did not get milked until almost noon. Friends helped the family carry their furniture back into the house. Their grandparents would have to live with them until the damage to the daudyhouse could be repaired. But they were thankful the fire had been no worse.

Shortly after noon the stream of visitors began. The girls thought it was jolly to eat all the fancy buns and tasty dishes that thoughtful friends and neighbors brought. Uncles, aunts, and cousins came to help put things back in order and bring more food.

The story of the fire was told over and over. Esther's part in it was told too.

"And Esther took the children out to the car and took care of them so that I could help here," Mother told the aunts. "She wrapped them up in blankets and got a bottle for the baby without even being told what to do."

"Good for you," the aunts said. "You did your part to save the house from burning."

"Esther is really brave," piped up Mary with admiring eyes for her big sister.

Mother looked at her daughter over the heads of the visitors, and they shared a secret smile.

24

Composition Theme

Our Daily Bread

Back of the loaf is the snowy flour,
  And back of the flour, the mill,
And back of the mill is the wheat and the shower,
  And the sun, and the Father's will.

MALTBIE D. BABCOCK

25

 # The Rescue

BY A SEA CAPTAIN

On a bright moonlit night in February 1831, when it was intensely cold, the little brig[1] that I commanded lay quietly at her anchors inside Sandy Hook. We had had a hard time, beating about for eleven days off the coast, with cutting northeasters blowing and snow and sleet falling for the most part of that time.

Forward, the vessel was thickly coated with ice. It had been hard work to handle her, as the rigging and sails were stiff and yielded only when the men exerted their strength to the utmost. When we finally made the port, all hands were worn down and exhausted.

"A bitter cold night, Mr. Larkin," I said to my mate as I tarried for a short time upon deck.

The worthy down-easter buttoned his coat more tightly around him, and looking up to the moon, he replied, "It's a whistler, captain; and nothing can live comfortably out of blankets tonight."

"The tide is running out swift and strong, and it will be well to keep a sharp lookout for floating ice, Mr.

---

[1]brig: a two-masted sailing ship

Larkin," said I as I turned to go below.

"Aye, aye, sir," responded the faithful mate.

About two hours afterward, I was aroused from a sound sleep by the vigilant officer. "Excuse me for disturbing you, captain," said he, "but I wish you would turn out and come on deck as soon as possible."

"What's the matter. Mr. Larkin?" said I.

"Why, sir, I have been watching a large cake of ice that swept by at a distance a moment ago; and I saw something black upon it, something that I thought moved. The moon is under a cloud, and I could not see clearly; but I believe there is a child floating out to the sea this freezing night on that cake of ice."

We were on deck before either spoke another word. The mate pointed out, with no little difficulty, the cake of ice floating off to the leeward,[2] with its white, glittering surface broken by a black spot. "Get the glass, Mr. Larkin," said I. "The moon will be out of that cloud in a moment, and then we shall see clearly."

I kept my eye upon the retreating mass of ice while the moon slowly worked its way through a heavy bank of clouds. Meantime the mate stood by me with the glass. When the full light fell upon the water with a brilliancy known only in our northern latitudes, I put the glass to my eye. One glance was enough.

"Forward, there!" I shouted at the top of my voice. With one bound I reached the ship's cutter[3] and began to cut away the ice-encrusted ropes that held it fast.

Mr. Larkin had taken the glass to look for himself. "There are *two* children on that cake of ice!" he exclaimed as he hurried to assist me in getting out the boat.

---

[2]leeward (lē′ wərd): the side of a ship sheltered from the wind
[3]cutter: a small boat carried on a larger boat and used to discharge passengers and freight, etc.

The men answered my call and walked quickly aft.[4] Very soon we launched the cutter, into which Mr. Larkin and I jumped, followed by two men who took the oars. I rigged the tiller,[5] and the mate sat beside me in the stern.

"Do you see that cake of ice with something black upon it, my lads? Put me alongside of that, and I'll give you a month's extra wages when you are paid off," said I to the men.

They bent to their oars, but their strokes were uneven and feeble, for they were worn out by the hard duty of the preceding fortnight. Though they did their best, the boat made little more headway than the tide. It was a losing chase, and Mr. Larkin, who was suffering torture as he saw how little we gained, cried out, *"Pull, lads! I'll double the captain's prize! Two month's extra pay! Pull, lads! Pull for life!"*

The men's desperate effort at the oars told how willing they were to obey, but their strength was gone. One of the poor fellows washed us twice in recovering his oar, and then he gave out. The other was nearly as far gone. Mr. Larkin sprang forward and seized the deserted oar. "Lie down in the bottom of the boat," said he to the men. "Captain, take the other oar. We must row for ourselves."

I took the second man's place. Larkin had stripped off his coat, and as he pulled the bow, I waited for the signal stroke. It came, and the next moment we were pulling a long, steady stroke, gradually increasing in tempo until the wood seemed to smoke in the oarlocks. We kept time, each by the long, deep breathing of the other.

Such a pull! We bent forward until our faces almost

[4]aft: the rear or stern of a vessel
[5]tiller: the handle on the rudder of a small boat

touched our knees; and then throwing all our strength into the backward movement, we drew on the oars until we gained every inch covered by the sweep. Thus we worked at the oars for fifteen minutes, though it seemed to me as many hours. The sweat rolled off in great drops, and I was enveloped in the steam rising from my own body.

"Are we almost up to it, Mr. Larkin?" I gasped out.

"Almost, captain," said he, "and don't give up! For the love of our dear little ones at home, don't give up, captain!"

The oars flashed as their blades turned up to the moonlight, for the men who plied them were fathers and had a father's heart.

Suddenly Mr. Larkin ceased pulling, and for a moment my heart almost stopped beating; for the terrible thought that his strength had given out. But I was reassured by his voice. "Gently, captain, gently. A stroke or two more. There, that will do!" The next moment Mr. Larkin sprang up on the ice. I called to the men to make fast the boat to the ice, and then I followed him.

We ran to the dark spot in the center of the mass and found two little boys. The head of the smaller was resting in the bosom of the larger. Both were fast asleep. They had been overcome by lethargy, which would have been fatal but for the timely rescue.

Mr. Larkin grasped one of the lads, tore off his jacket, and pulled off his shoes. Then loosening his own garments to the skin, he placed the cold child in contact with his own warm body, carefully wrapping his overcoat around him. I did the same with the other child, and we returned to the boat.

When we had the delight of restoring the children to their parents, we learned that they had been playing on the cake of ice, which had jammed into a bend of the river about ten miles above New York. A movement of the tide had set the ice in motion, and the little fellows were carried away that cold night and would have inevitably perished but for Mr. Larkin's sighting them as they were sweeping out to sea.

"How do you feel, Mr. Larkin?" I said to the mate the morning after this adventure.

"A little stiff in the arms, captain," the noble fellow replied. "A little stiff in the arms"—and laying his hand on his rough chest—"but very easy here."

26

 Hands That Shed
Innocent Blood

BY ELIZABETH WAGLER

Judge Louis folded his bejeweled hands and leaned across the council table, his small, glittering eyes glaring menacingly into the faces of his ten councilors.

"And what do you intend to do about the heretics?" he demanded.

The councilors of Znaym squirmed uneasily on their benches. One man pretended to see something outside the small window beside him; another drew his black cloak more closely about his shoulders; several crossed their legs or shuffled their feet; two or three cleared their throats. None of them dared to meet the gaze of the judge.

"Well," thundered Judge Louis impatiently, "I am waiting!"

Balthazar, the oldest of the councilors, raised his drawn, wrinkled face and spoke hesitantly. "They have been in prison for three weeks on bread and water, sir."

"Yes, yes, this I know already," snapped the judge.

The councilors remained strangely silent. Finally a large man among them, named Thomas, spoke up timidly "Perhaps they have been sufficiently punished and could be released shortly."

"Released?" Judge Louis rose slightly in his chair. "Released!" he shouted again. "You want to release those troublemakers?" His angry countenance caused most of the councilors to drop their eyes to the table.

Old Balthazar spoke again. "Pardon my boldness, sir, but may I point out that the three men and two women in question are not troublemakers. They have lived quiet and peaceable lives and have done no wrong."

"No wrong! No wrong, you say!" shouted Judge Louis furiously. "Is it not wrong to defy the imperial command of our new ruler, Archduke Ferdinand? He has decreed that every citizen must go to mass at the Holy Church at least once every month. These scoundrels have not entered the church or confessed to the priest for many years. Moreover, they have not had their infants baptized."

Balthazar rose unsteadily to his feet. He spoke carefully, "Sir Louis, and you, my fellow councilors, I beg you to consider what I say. We are Moravians. The prisoners are Moravians. They have dwelt among us for many years. They have worked with us, bought and sold among us. They have been kind and generous neighbors. True, they hold some strange beliefs. They do not enter our Holy Church but read the Bible in their homes. We all know this is a foolish thing for a common man to do, but it has not harmed anyone.

"Now, in this year of 1528, our beloved Moravia has come under the rule of Austria. This foreign monarch has given us new laws. But we, the Council of Znaym, are still rulers here. The king is far away. He is not likely to know or care what decisions we make. I recommend that we release the prisoners and leave them in peace. I wish no innocent blood on my hands." He bowed slightly to the judge and took his seat.

The other councilors had listened carefully. As Balthazar spoke, they nodded in agreement. Now they turned to Judge Louis for his reaction.

"So," the judge said grimly, "you are all traitors. You will not obey the decree that orders the destruction of Anabaptist heretics?"

"We are not traitors to Moravia or to our fellow men," replied Thomas.

"Then I will go myself to Austria and inform the Archduke Ferdinand of your disobedience. I will get a personal order from him for the destruction of these scoundrels!" The judge's face grew redder with each bold threat.

No one answered. The councilors were not intimidated. They stared stubbornly at the table top.

"You still will not condemn these people?" the judge demanded.

Slowly each man on the council shook his head. Not one was ready to see the Anabaptists killed.

Realizing that his threatened trip to Austria was quite impractical, Judge Louis rose abruptly to his feet. He paced before the council like a caged lion. "If you will not condemn the heretics to be burned," he thundered, "I will take it upon myself. I will draw the wood for the fire with my own horses and will personally set it alight!"

Old Balthazar spoke for all of them. "Sir Louis, we commend them to you; do with them as you please. It is committed to you."

Thus like Pilate of old, they sought to wash their hands of innocent blood.

Sir Louis was true to his word. The very next day, he had his servants haul a large quantity of wood to an open field outside the city. Five stout stakes were driven into the ground and the wood was piled around them.

The five Anabaptists were led out and burned there. They remained faithful unto death. Very few townspeople witnessed the execution, for most were sympathetic to the pious Christians.

Sir Louis, however, was not satisfied with the blood of these saints. He was determined to root out all heresy in his town. He offered a reward to any who would

inform him of the whereabouts of the brethren. He waited some weeks for an informer to appear. At last the temptation of a reward lured a town loafer to come with information.

One dark night Judge Louis assembled his forces. They included the informer, a bailiff, and several watchmen. The watchmen were not aware of who was to be arrested, but it was part of their duty to assist in apprehending criminals, so they came without question.

Stealthily the small group moved through the quiet street. "This is the house," whispered the informer, pointing to a brick building. "There are a dozen or more

Anabaptists inside, having a meeting."

"Ha! Good!" snorted Judge Louis. "Now we shall get a whole nest of them at once. Stand to the side," he commanded his men. "I will go first.

"It is so dark, I can hardly find the door," he muttered, fumbling along the wall with his hands.

"Shall I bring a light?" asked the bailiff.

"No, no," protested the judge. "I will just feel around for the door. There—it must be just over . . . a-a-a-a-ah—a-ah!" he screamed. There followed a dull thump. "O-o-o-o-oh, o-oh," he moaned pitifully, "O-oh, help! Help me out of here!"

The bailiff and the watchmen swarmed about in confusion. Their voices rose in excitement.

"Where are you?"

"Here, bring a light!"

"Let go of my cloak!"

"Can't find the lantern."

"Hurry. Get a light here!"

All the while, Judge Louis moaned and cursed loudly from somewhere beneath them.

The brethren inside the house heard the commotion and hurried out the back door. While they escaped to their homes, a crowd of aroused citizens gathered about the front of the building.

In the glow of the lanterns, the people saw that Judge Louis had stumbled into a hole made for lowering wine caskets into the cellar. He had injured his foot badly and was unable to walk. His servants carried him home and laid him in his bed.

By the next morning, the judge had a high fever, and he was suffering great agony from his broken foot. As the days passed, his pain increased and his fever continued. Nothing seemed to relieve his suffering, and he only grew worse. Between moans he cried out, "Oh, the Baptists, the Baptists." Over and over he repeated this cry.

Judge Louis never recovered from his injury. After his death, it became a common saying among the people of the region that he had been punished for shedding innocent blood.

"Thus saith the LORD; Execute ye judgment and righteousness, and deliver the spoiled out of the hand of the oppressor: and do no wrong, do no violence to the stranger, the fatherless, nor the widow, neither shed innocent blood in this place" (Jeremiah 22:3).

27

I Paused Last Eve

I paused last eve beside the blacksmith's door
  And heard the anvil's ring, the vesper's chime;
And looking in I saw upon the floor
  Old hammers, worn with beating years of time.
"How many anvils have you had?" said I,
  "To wear and batter all these hammers so?"
"Just one," he answered. Then with twinkling eye:
  "The anvil wears the hammers out, you know."
And so, I thought, the anvil of God's Word,
  For ages skeptics' blows have beat upon;
But though the noise of falling blows was heard,
  The anvil is unchanged; the hammers gone.

                                    JOHN CLIFFORD

28

Salmon Days

BY ELIZABETH WAGLER

July is an exciting time of the year for the native Indian children of north-central British Columbia. It is the time of the salmon run. Sockeye salmon, returning from their sojourn in the Pacific Ocean, swim in silver hordes up the Skeena River into the Babine Lake to spawn in the lake's many tributary streams. This is a story of how one family welcomes the salmon run.

PART I

Emma's eyes pop open suddenly, and she blinks in the bright sunlight streaming through the small window. Beside her, Mary, her little sister, sighs in her sleep and burrows deeper under the quilt. From the kitchen next to their room comes a sizzling sound and the fragrant aroma of frying fish.

Fish! Emma sits up with a jerk. She swings her legs over the edge of the bed and shakes her black hair back out of her eyes. In a few minutes she is racing through the kitchen toward the porch.

The glare of the sun on the glassy-smooth water of Lake Babine hurts her eyes. "Did Father leave for the sawmill yet?" Emma asks her mother, who has come to stand beside her on the porch.

"Oh, yes. You slept in. And the boys are already down at the boat."

"Are they?" Emma's voice is heavy with disappointment. "I wanted to be the first one out today." She leans far over the porch railing and peers toward the boat dock on the lake. There, George is untying the family's fourteen-foot wooden boat and Louis is loading the oars. Surely they are not planning to go without her. Emma dashes down the steps.

Mother calls after her, "Don't worry. The boys left in such a hurry that they forgot the tub for the fish. Do you think you could manage it?"

"Sure," Emma replies. "This is a good joke on them," she thinks as she scurries around the cabin to pull the big oblong fish tub from its nail on the back wall. "Why, this is the morning the boys hope to catch a hundred salmon! Where do they think they will stow a hundred slippery, flopping salmon if they have no fish tub? They beat me to the dock, but they will have to wait for me to bring the tub."

She struggles manfully down the steep trail, the clumsy tub almost too awkward for her thin, twelve-year-old arms.

Two days ago they set the net for the first time that year. The big fishnet, thirty feet long and eight feet wide and weighted with stones along the bottom edge, had been loaded carefully into the front of the boat. After selecting a likely spot, Mother had played out the net, hand over hand, while the boys steadied the boat against the gently rocking waves. Whenever Mother threw out the net, it seemed to unfold perfectly, Emma thought. The weights would disappear into the dark water one after the other in orderly succession. When the children tried it, however, the stones always managed to get tangled in the net and Mother would have to come to their rescue.

When the boys complained to Father about their difficulties in handling the big net, he sympathized, "I'm sure my big, clumsy fingers would get tangled too. Maybe that is why we men of the Skeena have always left the fishing to the women and children, eh? Just wait. Soon you boys will be men, and then you won't have to help with the salmon."

Emma is glad she is a girl. Fishing is hard work, but she enjoys the thrill of bringing in a net full of fish.

"You had to wait for me after all," Emma teases her brothers as she drags the big tub along the dock.

"Oh, we thought you might be useful," admits George, helping her into the boat with her burden. "Let's go!" He starts the small gas engine on the boat.

Out on the lake, George shuts off the engine and drops the anchor over the side. Next, he leans out to catch the floating stick that serves as a buoy to mark the end of the long net. "All together now, *heave!*" he calls. All three hook their fingers through the netting and pull.

"It's heavy," pants Louis, almost losing his balance in the rocking boat.

"Here they come," shouts Emma, leaning precariously over the side of the boat.

A flash of silver, and three entangled salmon flop into the boat. They average two feet in length and are still very much alive. In their struggles to escape, they have twisted themselves hopelessly in the net. While George balances himself on his feet and holds the net high, Louis untwists the snarls and Emma clasps the slippery fish in both hands and tosses them one by one into the fish tub.

Then they pull again. More salmon flop at their feet. Emma counts carefully as she throws them into the tub. It is a game. The most her mother ever took in one haul was 112, and it is exciting to see if the record can be broken.

They work steadily for almost an hour. Emma's arms begin to ache. Her stomach grumbles when she thinks of the fish her mother is frying at home.

"The lake is getting rough," George remarks as he shakes more salmon into the loaded boat.

"77 . . . 78 . . . 79 . . . ," chants Emma.

"How much net is still out?" asks Louis, looking at the tangled heap of netting sprawled around their feet.

"The other buoy is just over here." George points to a stick floating close beside them.

Small waves begin to slap against the boat, rocking it and almost upsetting George. The lake can become very rough with little warning, so the children know they must hurry. They strain their weary muscles and pull in the final length. A dozen fine fish come up in the net.

Leaving Emma and Louis to extract the last few salmon, George prepares to start the engine.

"Well, we didn't get a hundred," Emma sighs, perching herself on the edge of the overflowing tub. "I suppose Mother will be happy with ninety-one."

"Maybe next time," Louis says hopefully.

Catching the fish is only the first step. Now they must be cleaned and prepared for drying. Although fresh salmon is good, Emma considers it not nearly as delicious as Mother's smoked salmon.

PART II

After a late breakfast, Emma goes to the shore to watch Mother clean the fish. One quick chop, and the head is tossed into a large kettle. (Later, Mother will boil the heads to extract oil for use in tanning hides.) A neat slice of the knife; a few hard, precise scrapes with an old tablespoon; and the gutted fish is tossed into the shallow water of the lake to soak. *Chop, slice, flash* go the tools.

Mother hums a happy tune as she works. Emma's little sister Mary is splashing and squealing in the water. She lifts some of the cleaned salmon and drops them back with a splash.

"You'd better go help the boys," Mother suggests, and Emma starts down the beach to where the boys are washing and untangling the net. It is a complicated and wearisome job, but the sun is shining and the water is warm. Soon they are splashing each other and shouting gaily as they slosh the net up and down in the water.

"Here come the gulls!" shouts Emma suddenly, letting her end of the net trail in the lake as she points in the direction of the gathering flock.

Whirling and circling, their gleaming white bodies etched against the deep blue of the sky, a dozen sea gulls circle overhead. Screaming hoarsely, they swoop close to Mother and then soar upward again, only to double back and repeat the performance.

"Hey, Emma, let's hurry and get done," urge the boys. "Then we can feed them."

More and more gulls appear, attracted by the fish. Their harsh cries fill the air.

At last the net is neatly folded and the children splash toward Mother.

"You can take that pail and feed the gulls." Mother nods at a pailful of entrails, never pausing in her routine of *chop, slash, scrape.*

"I come too!" Mary scrambles, dripping, out of the water to grasp Emma's hand.

The hungry gulls follow the children to a point of land where they know they will be fed. Emma throws her hand up in alarm as one overeager bird almost plummets into her before making a neat turn and soaring skyward again.

Louis tosses the waste on the rocky shore, and the

124

children back away to watch the gulls descend on the feast. What a furious snatching and gobbling, screeching and flapping! Every year the children try to capture one of the white birds, but they are never quite fast enough.

Back in the yard, the children help to string the catch by their tails onto sharp, upright poles. There the cleaned fish will be left to dry in the sun.

PART III

By now it is midafternoon, and the family turns its attention to a long string of previously dried fish that must be prepared for smoking.

Emma is not as fast as Mother or the boys, but she tries to do her share. Standing before a board table, she lays each dried fish on its back and makes two long cuts on either side of the backbone. Then she makes a quick pull and throws the backbone under the table. Several more slits in the flesh make the salmon lie flat. Faster and faster her fingers fly as her pile of fish grows higher.

Mother is pleased. "These fish are nice and firm," she says. "We must hurry so that we can set the net again tonight."

Louis groans. He is getting tired of working on fish. "The fish will be running for two months yet. Why don't we take a rest for a day or two?" he asks.

Mother reminds him, "These first fish have made the journey quickly and are still fighting strong, Louis. The later ones will be so weak by the time they get here that their flesh will be mushy and half rotten. That is why we have to set the nets again tonight. We'll stop when we have our winter's supply."

Late in the afternoon, Mother and the children transfer the now boneless fish to the wooden smokehouse under the poplar trees. They drape them carefully over the slender poles. "Like towels on a wash line," says Emma. Mother stirs the small fire in the sunken fire pit on the dirt floor. Soon thick clouds of smoke are swirling around the hanging meat, and the children retreat from the smokehouse, choking and sputtering. Mother backs after them, her hand over her face. She closes and bolts the wooden door firmly.

The slow birch fire will be kept burning as more and more fish are hung over the poles. This summer Mother hopes to smoke at least five hundred salmon for the family's use and as many more to sell to the fish buyers who come to their village.

Emma skips through the grove of poplar trees beside the smokehouse and ducks under a small verminproof wooden cache standing on spindly stilts above the ground. In another six weeks it will be filled with stacks and stacks of hard, dry salmon waiting to be eaten in the cold winter days. Emma can almost taste them already.

She walks, tired and happy, up the path to the house. Tonight they will set the net again. Maybe tomorrow they will catch a hundred salmon.

29

 Susan's Temptation

BY MRS. EMBURY

One Saturday evening, Susan went as usual to Farmer Thompson's inn to receive the price of her mother's washing for the boarders. She found the farmer in the stable yard. He was apparently in a terrible rage with some horse dealers with whom he was bargaining. In his hand he had an open pocketbook full of bills; and scarcely noticing the child as she made her request, he handed her the payment.

Glad to escape so easily, Susan hurried through the gate. Then pausing to pin the money safely in the folds of her shawl, she discovered that Farmer Thompson had given her two bills instead of one—twice the amount that was due! She looked around; nobody was near to share her discovery, and her first feeling was joy at the unexpected prize.

"It is mine—all mine," she said to herself. "I will buy Mother a new cloak with it, and she can give her old one to my sister Mary. Then Mary can go to Sunday school with me next winter. I wonder if it will not buy a pair of shoes for brother Tom too?"

At that moment Susan remembered that Farmer Thompson must have given the extra money to her by mistake, and therefore she had no right to it. But the voice of the tempter whispered, "He gave it, and how do you know that he did not intend to make you a present of it? Keep it. He will never know. Even if it is a mistake, he had too many bills in that great pocketbook to miss one."

While this conflict was going on in her mind, Susan was hurrying home as fast as possible, all the while balancing the comforts that the money would buy against the sin of wronging her neighbor. It seemed the balance was tipped in favor of the comforts.

As she crossed the little bridge before her home, her eyes fell upon a garden seat that she and her mother had often occupied. It was there, only the day before, that her mother had explained to her those words of Scripture: "Whatsoever ye would that men should do to you, do ye even so to them."

Startled, as if a trumpet had sounded in her ears, Susan turned suddenly around, and as though flying from some unseen peril, she hastened back along the road with breathless speed. She found herself once more at Farmer Thompson's gate.

"What do you want now?" he asked gruffly as she approached him.

"Sir, you paid me two bills instead of one," Susan said, trembling in every limb.

"Two bills, did I? Let me see. Well, so I did! But did you just find it out? Why did you not bring it back sooner?"

Susan blushed and hung her head.

"You wanted to keep it, I suppose," he said, "Well, I am glad your mother is more honest than you, or I should have been five dollars poorer and none the wiser."

"My mother knows nothing about it, sir," Susan

replied. "I brought it back before I went home."

The old man looked at the child, and seeing the tears rolling down her cheeks, he seemed touched by her distress. Putting his hand in his pocket, he drew out a shilling and offered it to her.

"No, sir, I thank you," she sobbed. "I do not want to be paid for doing right. I only wish you would not think me dishonest, for indeed it was a great temptation. Oh, sir! If you have ever seen those you love best wanting the common comforts of life, you must know how hard it is for us to always do unto others as we would have others do unto us."

The heart of the selfish man was moved. "There be things which are little upon the earth, but they are exceedingly wise," he murmured as he bade the little girl good night and entered his house.

Susan returned to her home with a lightened heart. Through the course of a long and useful life, she never forgot the great temptation she faced that day.

30

Our Refuge and Strength

All: God is our refuge and strength,
    A very present help in trouble.

Boys: Therefore will not we fear,
    Though the earth be removed,
    And though the mountains be carried
    Into the midst of the sea;

Girls: Though the waters thereof roar and be troubled,
    Though the mountains shake with the swelling
    thereof.

All: Selah.

Solo boy: There is a river,
    The streams whereof shall make glad
    The city of God,

Solo girl: The holy place of the tabernacles
    Of the most High.

All: God is in the midst of her;
    She shall not be moved:
    God shall help her,
    And that right early.

    Girls: The heathen raged, the kingdoms were moved:
              He uttered his voice, the earth melted.

      All: The LORD of hosts is with us;
              The God of Jacob is our refuge.
              Selah.

    Boys: Come, behold the works of the LORD,
              What desolations he hath made in the earth.

Solo boy: He maketh wars to cease
              Unto the end of the earth;

Solo girl: He breaketh the bow,
              And cutteth the spear in sunder;

Solo boy: He burneth the chariot in the fire.

    Girls: Be still, and know that I am God:
              I will be exalted among the heathen,
              I will be exalted in the earth.

      All: The LORD of hosts is with us;
              The God of Jacob is our refuge.
              Selah.

PSALM 46

31

A Mother Bear Story

BY M. J. BAER

The summer sun moves on its way and will soon
sink below the horizon to bring another day to its
close. Mother Bear is enjoying herself in Farmer
Brown's oats field.

She loves oats in the milk stage and delights in strip-
ping the fat kernels from their stalks. A wary animal,
she often rises to make a hasty survey of her surroundings. When erect, Mother Bear stands about five feet
tall. Unfortunately, in her quest for succulent grain, she
destroys much more than she eats, trampling it down
with her two-hundred-pound bulk.

At length she has had enough and ambles off into
the forest, and soon she emerges in a nearby sheep pasture. Her arrival does not go unnoticed. Startled sheep
make a headlong dash toward safety. Their owner,
enjoying the sunset from his back porch, loses no time
in running for his rifle. Although he realizes that black
bears do not present a great threat to livestock, he is not
taking any chances. Before he can return with his rifle,
however, Mother Bear has disappeared. The sheep

rancher chuckles to think that she was probably as startled by the panicking sheep as they were by her unannounced arrival.

Although Mother Bear will eat almost anything, she is not extremely fond of domestic animals. Small wild animals, if they can be caught, will sometimes tempt her, as will the carcasses of larger game. But more than these, she loves honey and will clean out any beehive she finds—bees, honey, and all! She also enjoys berries and delights in eating the wild ones that grow on secluded, sunny mountain slopes.

With the advance of autumn, Mother Bear follows a salmon stream in search of the remains of salmon that have died after spawning. She gorges herself along the river bank and grows very sleek and fat. Instinct has given her an enormous appetite at this time of year. She must store up fat for her long sleep, which will begin in late November.

When the days grow shorter and the weather gets colder, she starts another quest. It is now time to seek a winter home. Before long she finds a hollow beneath the roots of a large conifer on the north slope of a mountain. Mother Bear always seeks a den on a north slope away from the direct rays of the sun. Its warmth could play havoc with the stable atmosphere of her den by melting the snow away from its entrance too early.

Satisfied that she has found a suitable place to give birth to her young, Mother Bear begins to make a den large enough for her overstuffed body. She allows extra space to accommodate what could be as many as three babies. With her work finally done, she settles for a long sleep.

As she slumbers, strange things happen to her body. Some of the normal functions of her body cease or slow down. She sleeps on and on, kept strong by the fat she has stored through the summer and autumn.

On a bleak, cold day in February, the entire land-scape is host to a soft blanket of snow. All is still and quiet. But an exciting event has taken place beneath the cedar tree—Mother Bear has awakened from her slumber long enough to give birth to twin cubs. Weighing hardly one pound each and born without any hair, they present quite a contrast to their well-insulated mother.

We might think that these little ones would find themselves born into a cold and inhospitable world. Not so! God has provided for the comfort of all His creatures. Snuggled close to their mother and drawing from her abundant supply of milk, they are as content as one could imagine. Meanwhile, Mother sleeps on.

The days lengthen more and more. The course of the sun takes it higher overhead until the day is as long as the night, which means another spring has come. The snow that is lying in the forest begins to melt. Small patches of bare earth show here and there. The waters of the melting snow form small streams that wind down mountainsides to cascade into rivers below.

Before long, sprigs of early vegetation begin to peep through the forest floor. Now Mother Bear becomes rest-less; her long sleep is drawing to a close. Finally, with the coming of April, she pushes her way out of the den, followed by two little black balls of fur. The search for food begins anew. Now Mother Bear has three mouths to feed! Her first meal consists of some wild parsnips that have lived through the winter under the snow.

The cubs are now about the size of house cats and are as playful and mischievous as kittens. It is intriguing to watch Mother Bear care for them. She sometimes pad-dles them the same way our mothers find it necessary to paddle us. They will live with her for about two years before they are sent out on their own. During this time,

Mother Bear will teach them how to find their own food and care for themselves.

And this brings us to the end of our Mother Bear story, except for a few words of advice. When a mother bear is caring for little ones, she can be very fierce, and will not hesitate to attack any man or beast that she thinks may harm her babies. It is extremely dangerous to get between a mother bear and her cubs. Most of the stories we hear of bears attacking humans are stories of mother bears trying to protect their little ones.

Many people who do not understand bears put themselves in a danger by feeding them in our national parks. Bears are best observed from safe and distant observation points, however, and this is the reason that along park roads there are signs forbidding us to feed the bears. We should respect the God-given instincts of bears as well as all the animals that live in our lands and forests.

John Maynard

BY J. B. GOUGH

John Maynard was well known in the Lake district as a God-fearing, honest, and intelligent pilot. He was pilot on a steamboat from Detroit to Buffalo. One summer afternoon, when the boat was not far out of Buffalo and John Maynard was at the helm, smoke began rising from the hold. The captain, who was in the bridge with the pilot, called out, "Simpson, go below, and see what is the matter down there."

Simpson came up with his face pale as ashes and said, "Captain, the ship is on fire."

Then, "Fire! Fire! Fire on shipboard!"

All hands were called up. Buckets of water were dashed on the fire, but in vain. There were large quantities of rosin and tar on board, and it was found impossible to save the ship. The passengers, startled by this turn of events, asked the captain, "How far are we from Buffalo?"

"Seven miles."

"How long before we can reach there?"

"Three-quarters of an hour at our present rate of steam."

"Is there any danger?"

"Yes, there is danger. See the smoke bursting out! Go forward if you would save your lives."

Passengers and crew—men, women, and children—crowded the forward part of the ship. (At that time, steamers seldom carried lifeboats.) John Maynard stood at the helm. The flames burst forth in a sheet of fire; clouds of smoke arose. The captain, who was trying to keep the desperate passengers and crew from abandoning ship, cried out through his trumpet, "John Maynard!"

"Aye, aye, sir!"

"Are you at the helm?"

"Aye, aye, sir!"

"How does she head?"

"Southeast by east, sir."

"Head her southeast and run her on shore," said the captain.

Nearer, nearer, yet nearer, she approached the shore. Again the captain cried out, "John Maynard!"

The response came feebly this time, "Aye, aye, sir!"

"Can you hold on five minutes longer, John?" he said.

"By God's help, I will."

The man's hair was burned from his scalp. But with one hand disabled and his other hand upon the wheel, he stood firm as a rock. And he beached the ship.

Every man, woman, and child was saved—except John Maynard.

Perseverance

One step and then another,
  And the longest walk is ended;
One stitch and then another,
  And the largest rent in mended.

One brick upon another,
  And the highest wall is made;
One flake upon another,
  And the deepest snow is laid.

So little coral workers,
  By their slow and constant motion,
Have built those pretty islands.
  In the distant dark blue ocean.

And the noblest undertakings
  Man's wisdom has conceived,
By oft-repeated effort,
  Have been patiently achieved.

Then do not look disheartened
  On the work you have to do,
And say that such a mighty task
  You never can get through;

138

But just endeavor day by day
    Another point to gain,
And soon the mountain which you feared
    Will prove to be a plain.

Rome was not builded in a day,
    The ancient proverb teaches;
And Nature, by her trees and flowers,
    The same sweet sermon preaches.

Think not of far-off duties,
    But of duties which are near;
And, having once begun to work,
    Resolve to persevere.

AUTHOR UNKNOWN

Mary's Bible

REVISED AND REWRITTEN BY MARY CARTER

This is a true story about a young girl, Mary Jones, who wanted very much to have a Bible of her own. But in the year 1802, Bibles were rare and very costly in Wales, which is where our story takes place. It was not until a number of years after Mary received her Bible that Mr. Charles (whom you will meet in this story) was able to persuade a group of concerned men that the Welsh people desperately needed more Bibles printed in their own tongue. It is believed that the account of Mary Jones and her Bible played a considerable part in bringing this about.

Our story begins on the day that Mary was to set out for Bala, a village twenty-five miles from her own, to purchase her very own Bible.

PART I

That morning Mary left her bed at dawn. It was to be the most important day in her life. After working and saving for six years, this was the day she was going for her Bible!

Her parents were already preparing a meal for her in the living room below, and after they had eaten and drunk together, they all knelt and prayed for blessing and protection for Mary on her great adventure. Then, after kissing her parents and slinging a small satchel containing her provisions over her shoulder, Mary went out barefoot into the early spring morning.

As she walked along the soft turf by the wayside, she could hear a song thrush fluting in a tree. Rabbits, not expecting human folk to be abroad so early, sat up and looked at her, then loped away into their burrows. The mountains, especially Cader Idris, the loftiest of the peaks, looked soft and friendly in the sunshine. Mary looked up at their broad slopes and rocky crags.

"They look almost protecting today," she thought, "as if they know I am going all by myself on a long journey, and they are taking care of me."

The words of Psalm 121 came into her mind.

" 'I will lift up mine eyes unto the hills, from whence cometh my help,' " she sang. "That will be my psalm for today. It so suits me. 'My help cometh from the LORD, which made heaven and earth. He will not suffer thy foot to be moved: he that keepeth thee will not slumber.' How safe and happy I feel when I think of those words. 'The LORD is thy keeper: the LORD is thy shade upon thy right hand. The sun shall not smite thee by day, nor the moon by night. The LORD shall preserve thee from all evil: he shall preserve thy soul. The LORD shall preserve thy going out and thy coming in from this time forth, and even for evermore.' "

Mary quickened her step.

" 'The LORD shall preserve thee from all evil,' " she repeated, "and I am going for my Bible! I am really on my way to get my own Bible! I can hardly believe it, even yet."

At first the way led over familiar ground, and she had a sense of being near to her home. But soon she passed into unknown country where there was little sign of habitation. The path led upward from the base of Cader Idris. Here and there, tucked into a fold in the hills, she saw a lonely farmhouse or caught sight of a shepherd and his dog high up on a neighboring slope; but for the rest she was the only moving figure in the whole vast, empty landscape. The track grew wilder as she climbed the shoulder of the mountain, and Mary had to scramble over boulders and sometimes make quite long detours where the path was blocked by a fall of rock. She stuck to it gamely and at last was rewarded. She came to the brow of a hill and looked down on the valley beneath.

It had been a tiring climb, and as she stood gazing round her, she seemed utterly alone on the bare shoulder of the mountain. Fold after fold of lesser hills rolled away under her feet on every side. The world looked very big, and she felt very small. Suddenly her enterprise loomed up before her as something beyond her strength, and she felt the clutch of panic at her heart. Somewhere in the distance lay the little town of Bala—and her Bible. But she had already walked a long way. How much farther must she go, and what would be her fate at the end of the journey?

She stood poised, unable to move, a prey for the first time to doubt. Then she looked again at the hills and at Cader Idris stretching up behind and beyond her. " 'I will life up mine eyes unto the hills. . . . My help cometh from the LORD, which made heaven and earth.' " Slowly courage flowed back into her, and she stepped forward toward the valley with a lighter heart.

It was easier going now, and the track wound down the mountainside into the trees of a wood. Presently the trees gave place to cultivated land, and farms appeared more frequently. To her right lay a tiny hamlet, and

Mary's spirits rose as she came again within sight of the dwellings of men.

Presently she saw a gate leading into a grassy field.

"I will go in and sit on the grass," she thought, "and have some dinner."

She entered the gate and found a sheltered place by a hedge. On every side the lovely hills surrounded her.

"I can lift up mine eyes unto the hills while I eat," she thought.

So she rested and enjoyed the lovely scene while she ate her dinner. Then she found a little wayside stream rippling over clean, washed stones, and she took a drink and bathed her face and hands. Then, rested and refreshed, she went on her way.

It was now afternoon, and the sun was hot. The way stretched along a dusty road, and Mary felt her bare feet grow sore and tired as she plodded on. Once she saw a woman standing in a cottage garden, who looked kindly over the hedge at her.

"Is it very far to Bala, ma'am?" Mary asked.

"Oh, a long way," the woman answered. "Many miles. Are you going to Bala? You look hot and tired, child. Sit on that bench and rest a minute, and I will bring you some buttermilk."

"Thank you, ma'am," said Mary gratefully. She rested while the good woman went and fetched the buttermilk, which she brought to Mary in a gaily painted mug. Mary thought the buttermilk was the most delicious she had ever tasted. She was sure she had never been so tired and thirsty in her life before.

"Have you come from far, child?" asked the kindly woman. "I don't seem to know you."

"I have come from Llanfihangel," answered Mary. "It's a long way away, near Abergynolwyn; and as you say that Bala is many miles from here, I think I must hurry on. I thank you very kindly for the buttermilk."

"Yes," agreed the woman, "you must get there before dark."

Mary walked quickly on again. The woman's remark about getting to Bala before dark rather alarmed her. To be benighted in this strange place was different from running about the familiar paths in the dark at home. The shadows were growing long when Mary saw a young girl sitting at the door of a little farm, eating her supper.

"Is it very far to Bala?" Mary asked her.

"No, not far," the girl answered. "It is just down the hill. Have you walked far? I am having my supper out here because it is so hot in the kitchen. Come and have supper with me. I am sure you must be hungry."

"Thank you," said Mary. "Yes, I am hungry, and tired. I have come from near Abergynolwyn today."

"All that way!" exclaimed the farmer's daughter. "You must be a good walker. Here, take a piece of cheese."

"We never go out for walks," continued the girl. "It is all work, work, work, on the farm here."

"Oh, I work very hard too," Mary answered quietly.

"Megan," called a voice from the kitchen. "Haven't you finished your supper yet? It's almost time for chores."

"There, Mother is calling!" exclaimed the girl. "I must go in. It is not far to Bala now. Good night."

"Good night, and thank you very much," said Mary. She went on her way with a glad heart.

Lights were shining from some of the windows of Bala as Mary walked down the hill. She could see a great lake gleaming softly in the dim light. It all seemed very beautiful. Mary's first care when she entered the little town was to find the house of the preacher. Her pastor in Llanfihangel had directed her there, promising that he would be sure to help her purchase a Bible.

"Can you tell me where Pastor David Edwards lives?"

Mary asked a woman who was coming out of a house.

"Yes," answered the woman. "I am going that way; I will show you."

The Welsh people are ever willing to direct a stranger, even if it means going out of their way to do so. Mary and her new friend chatted as they walked along the street, and soon the woman pointed to a house across the way.

"That is where Pastor Edwards lives," she informed the girl. "Oh, that is nothing, you are welcome," the woman said in answer to Mary's thanks. "Good evening."

Mary knocked at Pastor Edwards' door, and the pastor himself answered. He looked a little puzzled at his late visitor until Mary told him that Pastor Huw from her village had recommended that she come to him. Then he invited her in and listened with the kindest interest to her story.

"You must certainly see Mr. Charles," he said, "but not tonight; it is too late. I will take you to him tomorrow morning. He rises early, for he is such a busy gentleman, and I am sure he will gladly do what he can for you. You may sleep here. My wife will prepare the guest's bed."

It was not long before a tired Mary was shown to her room, and after a short prayer of thanksgiving for her safe journey, she stretched her weary limbs in the bed. The psalm that had been her companion all the day returned to her mind again, and she repeated it as she rested.

"He that keepeth me will not slumber," she thought. "No, I am safe. And I am going to get my Bible tomorrow." With that she fell happily asleep.

PART II

Only a dusky light was showing at Mary's bedroom window when Pastor Edwards knocked at her door.

"Mary Jones," he called. "are you awake? I can see a

light in Mr. Charles's window. He is busy at his desk already, I expect, so we can go over and see him."

"Thank you, Mr. Edwards, I will come at once," answered Mary, and she hurriedly but carefully washed and dressed. She knelt for a few minutes in prayer, and then she came down to the Edwards' sitting room, where Pastor Edwards and his wife were waiting for her.

"Take a drink of hot milk, child," said Mrs. Edwards, noticing the Mary was trembling ever so slightly.

Breakfast over, Mary and the pastor went out and crossed the street to the house where Mr. Charles lived. Pastor Edwards knocked softly, and presently Mr. Charles opened the door.

"Ah, good morning, friend Edwards," said Mr. Charles. "This is an early visit indeed. Nothing wrong, I hope."

"No, sir," answered Pastor Edwards, "nothing wrong, but a very important matter. I saw the light in your window and ventured to come over, as this young girl has come far to make a request."

"Come in, come in," said Mr. Charles.

The pastor and Mary followed him. Mary was nervous and trembling at the thought of being so close to getting her Bible.

"Sit down, Mr. Edwards," said Mr. Charles as they entered the study, "and tell me what has happened." He had noted Mary's poor clothing and roughened hands, and was expecting to hear a petition for work or other help of some kind.

"Nothing wrong has happened, Mr. Charles," repeated the pastor gravely. "But this young girl, Mary Jones, has walked all the way from Llanfihangel, near Abergynolwyn, to ask if you have a Bible you can spare for her."

"A Bible!" said Mr. Charles, interested at once. "Tell me, child, can you read?"

"Oh, yes, sir," answered Mary. "I have not long left Abergynolwyn School.

"Do you live with your parents?" asked Mr. Charles.

"Yes, sir," answered Mary, feeling much more at ease now that she was speaking of her own home. "My father and mother are weavers."

"Now tell me," said Mr. Charles, "how is it that you have made this long journey in order to buy a Bible? Do you know anything of the Scriptures?"

"Yes, sir," answered Mary, her eyes shining. "I love the Bible. I have loved it ever since I was a little girl and heard it read at meetings when I went with my mother and father. Then the school opened, when I was ten, and I learned to read; and a Sunday school started too, and I went. I needed a Bible more than ever then, and a kind friend, Mrs. Evans, promised that when I could read, I could go and study her Bible at her farm. So I went every Saturday to study my Sunday school lesson."

"Does Mrs. Evans live in Llanfihangel?" asked Mr. Charles.

"No," Mary answered. "Her farm is up the mountain, two miles away."

"And you walked two miles every Saturday to study the Scriptures," said Mr. Charles. "Indeed! And what do you remember of the Scriptures now? Can you repeat a psalm?"

"Yes, sir," said Mary, "I know many psalms: 'The LORD is my shepherd'; and I love Psalm 104: 'Bless the LORD, O my soul'—all about the rocky hills, and the birds and trees. But coming up from Llanfihangel yesterday, the psalm 'I will lift up mine eyes unto the hills' was in my mind all the time. It seemed to be my own psalm, specially for me."

Mary's face glowed, and her dark eyes shone as she spoke. Both the pastor and Mr. Charles were touched at her deep, unaffected feeling.

"Do you know any part of the Gospels?" asked Mr. Charles.

"Oh, yes, sir," Mary answered. "I can tell most of the parables. I used to teach the neighbors' children when I took them out on the moor. And I know most of the Sermon on the Mount. The seventh chapter was the first part I ever learned."

"And you have come all the way from Llanfihangel to buy a Bible," reflected Mr. Charles.

"Yes, if you please, sir," Mary put in quietly. "I have the money here in this purse."

"But if your parents are weavers, and not very rich, as I would suppose, how could you get so much money as a Bible, alas, now costs?" asked Mr. Charles.

"I worked and saved for six years," Mary answered. "I minded children. I did mending for neighbors. I picked sticks. I kept chickens—oh, I did everything I could to save enough."

Mr. Charles sat in silence for a time; then he turned to the pastor.

"Oh, friend Edwards!" he exclaimed. "Is not this too unutterably sad? To see this young girl, so brave, so intelligent, so consistent a Christian, coming all this long twenty-five miles to me for a Bible, and I have none to spare for her, not one. And there is no hope of getting one, for the Society has refused to print any more for Wales!"

"And have you nothing for this poor child, Mr. Charles?" faltered Pastor Edwards.

"I have not one," answered Mr. Charles. "There are two or three Bibles in that bookcase, but they are promised to others. I have none to spare."

As Mr. Charles spoke, his words fell like stones on Mary's ears. She gave a low cry and stretched out her hands as if she was about to fall. A black despair seemed to envelop her like a cloud. All the years of working, waiting, and hoping seemed to rise up like a great wave that would engulf her and sweep her way. It had all been for nothing! The long, weary walk yesterday had been a fool's errand. How happy she had been yesterday! So full of hope—but all for nothing.

At this last thought Mary's feelings gave way, and she burst into wild, uncontrollable weeping. Burying her face in her hands, she sank into a chair, for her frame shook so much that she could not stand. Her surroundings and the two ministers sitting in grave silence were forgotten in the overwhelming sorrow that possessed her. She must go back *without* her Bible!

Suddenly Mr. Charles rose from his chair and laid his hand on Mary's head.

"My child," he said. "You *shall* have your Bible. I cannot send you away empty, no matter who else goes short. Calm yourself, my child."

Mr. Charles went to the bookcase, and opening a door, he brought out a Bible and returned to Mary's side.

"Take it, Mary," he said, putting it into her hands. Mary held the Bible in her hands. She looked up at him, her eyes still brimming with tears but the light of hope shining in her face.

"Is it really for me?" she whispered.

"It is for you, my child," said Mr. Charles. "A just reward for all your earnest work and trust. May God bless you in your reading of it, and may it be the comfort you deserve. Oh, friend Edwards," he went on, turning to the pastor, "and this in only one illustration of the terrible need for the Bible in Wales! I will never rest until something is done to relieve this want."

Mary rose now, and after faltering her thanks to Mr. Charles, she walked to the door, her Bible clasped in her arms. Her one desire was to return to her parents and show them her treasure. After a hasty meal with her new friends, Pastor and Mrs. Edwards, she set out on her walk home.

It was later in the morning than the hour at which she had started the day before, but it was a cool, blustering day; a good day for walking. Mary passed over mile after mile of road as though in a dream. Holding her Bible clasped to her breast, her head erect and a smile on her face, she went on, unconscious of everything around her. She had her Bible, her *own* Bible, and she was on her way home! Weariness, hunger, and thirst went unnoticed.

She did notice the girl who had shared her supper with her the evening before, and they waved to each other, for the farm girl was going across a field to the cows. Mary also remembered the cottage and the kind old lady who had given her buttermilk, but the door was shut. The weather was too rough for the old woman to be gardening today. But casual passers-by on the road, though they would see the happy look on the girl's face and would wish her "good day," were unheeded by Mary; her thoughts were too full. Some would turn and look after her, murmuring, "I wonder what makes her look so happy."

Once, Mary sat for half an hour or so and rested while she ate some food that Mrs. Edwards had given her. Then she was up and away again.

Soon the dear, familiar Cader Idris was in view. It was some hours, though, before Mary climbed its foothills. After a last scramble over the shoulder of the friendly mountain, she reached home ground.

Dusk was falling, and Mr. and Mrs. Jones sat listening in the cottage, their looms silent.

"It will be getting dark soon," said Mrs. Jones.

"Aye," returned Jacob quietly. "Mary knows her way in the dark." Then almost under his breath, he added, "Twenty-five miles in one day!"

Mrs. Jones looked out the window, then turned to the fire and stirred some soup on the hob.

"Hark!" exclaimed her husband.

They listened. The gate latch clicked and a quick, light footstep came up the path. The door opened and Mary came in. Mrs. Jones stood trembling, unable to speak; but Mary's father stretched out his arms to her. In a voice deep with emotion, he spoke almost unconsciously the words of the prophet. " 'Is it well with the child?' "

Mary went straight to him. " 'It is well,' " she replied in perfect content.

"My dear," said Mrs. Jones now. "You have your Bible?"

For an answer, Mary turned to her mother with a soft radiance in her face and laid the Bible in her hands.

"Thanks be to God!" the mother breathed.

She gazed at the Bible for a few moments; then giving it to her husband, she turned toward the fire again.

"Come, my dear," she said, "you must be worn out. Come and have some food; that must be the first thing. Father, we will let Mary eat and rest first. Then she can tell us how everything went and what has happened in these two long days, and we can see the Bible properly."

When Mary had some food and rest, there seemed no end to the story she had to tell her parents; and of course, the smallest happening was important in their eyes. At last, though it was late at night, she opened her Bible, and they all looked at it with reverent love. Mary's Bible! It seemed too good to be true. Mary felt as if she had suddenly acquired an extensive library, so scarce were books in those days, and this was the Book of books!

"How lovely to have the Bible itself," Mary said.

"Yes," agreed her father, "and now you are needing a long rest, Mary. But I don't think we could go to bed satisfied if we did not have a few words from the Holy Bible. Read something, Mary, and then let us thank God for all His mercies."

Mary opened her Bible and turned the pages for a few moments. Then, with a thrill in her voice, she read Psalm 150.

" 'Praise ye the LORD. Praise God in his sanctuary: praise him in the firmament of his power.' " And when she came to the last verse, " 'Let every thing that hath breath praise the LORD. Praise ye the LORD,' " her voice rose in triumph.

Rising from their seats with one accord, the family knelt together and gave thanks to God. Then with deep joy and peace in her heart, Mary wished her parents good night and went up to her little room.

35

 The Oil or the Book

AUTHOR UNKNOWN

Zaidan, a girl of the Bagobo tribe, stepped down the ladder from her bark house in the hills near Davao on Mindanao of the Philippines. Her light brown skin was clean from a bath in the cold stream that flowed from the hills to the plains where the lowlanders lived.

Down the ladder after Zaidan came her mother and her little brother. They too were fresh from a bath in the stream and wore clean clothes of coarsely woven striped cotton.

With sure, free strides the three walked the rough mountain trail that led past all the bark huts of their Bagobo barrio in the hills. They hardly noticed the beautiful view from the clearings. They lived every day with the beauty of tropical vines, trees, flowers, and birds.

"Mother," Zaidan began the question that was bothering her. "Where is Father? Will he come to church with us?"

"We cannot wait for him." Zaidan's mother did not seem ready to answer her daughter's question. She added something that seemed to give her a little comfort.

"Anyway, he has been baptized."

"He was baptized," agreed Zaidan. "But after a few times he did not go to church anymore. Where does he go now? He is away from home for many hours. Where does he go?"

Zaidan's mother did not answer. It was her father that answered. After a few more steps along the trail they saw him. He was in a clearing in front of one of the high bark houses, squatting on the ground in a circle of other men from the Bagobo tribe. In front of them was a flicker of lighted wick burning in coconut oil. The men were droning a pagan chant in worship of the oil.

Zaidan's little brother ran to his father and squatted on the ground beside him. He stared at the flame as he saw the men doing. With a little cry of horror, his mother picked up her child and swung him to her shoulder. Then she grasped Zaidan by the hand. Together they hurried along the trail toward the church, which stood in the next barrio.

Zaidan was ready to cry. She had been so happy when her father had been baptized into their church. For weeks he had been kinder and happier than she had ever seen him. He took better care of his family. But lately things had changed again. He was away from home more, and when he was at home, he was no longer kind and pleasant. Now Zaidan knew why he was different. He had gone back to the pagan worship.

"Why?" was all Zaidan could think as she ran to keep up with her mother's long steps. "Why?"

Her mother understood what she wanted to ask. "I think it is because he is proud and cannot read. He has been ashamed that he does not know enough to hold the hymnbook right side up. He is ashamed that he cannot answer questions in the class of new members.

"When the pastor tells us what to study in the Bible,

we cannot. It is impossible to remember everything we hear. We should read it again in order to learn. But we cannot read.

"To worship the oil, your father does not need to learn anything new. He does not even need to think. He feels that he must worship something, so he takes the easy way."

Zaidan understood. She knew how it felt to be behind her class in the public school because she missed so many days.

"I'll try harder to learn at school," she promised. "I'll go every day and study hard. Then I can teach you and Father how to read."

"That will be good." Her mother almost smiled again. "Let's hope you can teach us before it is too late."

They were in sight of their church now, built on its posts high above the ground that was wet so much of the time. Its roof was of dried cogon grass, its walls and floors of bamboo. They saw a young man, a stranger, going in the door with the pastor. He was a lowlander, not one of the Bagobo tribe. They could tell by the way he dressed.

Zaidan, her mother, and her little brother sat on one of the wooden benches near the back of the church. The service began as usual. Soon the pastor introduced the visitor, a student from Silliman University who was going to spend his vacation in their hills. When Zaidan heard what he was going to do for them, she could hardly hold herself from jumping on her bench and clapping her hands and shouting for joy.

"Anybody who wants to learn to read can come to the church every day. There will be classes every morning and every evening," the new young man was explaining. "Do not think it will be too hard for you. Do not think you are too old, or too tired. We have an easy way to learn—just a few words at a time from big charts with pictures. Soon you will be able to read from primers, then from storybooks written especially for you, then from your hymnbooks and Bibles."

On the way home from church, Zaidan ran ahead of her mother. She wanted to be the first to tell her father that he could learn to read.

There is not time to tell everything that happened in that little Bagobo barrio in the hills that summer. We must skip to the end of the story, which you have probably guessed already.

It is a Sunday morning a few months later. Zaidan, Sunday-clean, again comes down the ladder from her bark house. This time she is followed by her mother and her little brother *and* her father, all just as Sunday-clean as Zaidan from their baths in the cold mountain stream.

Together they walk past the bark huts of their barrio in the hills. They walk down the trail to the place where the men are squatting on the ground, chanting in worship of the oil that burns in front of them. Zaidan's father greets his neighbors politely. He tells them where he is going. But he does not so much as glance at the flame. With steady strides he leads his family along the trail to the church of bamboo and cogon.

Inside, they follow him down the aisle to one of the front benches. Sitting between their parents, Zaidan and her little brother watch them pick up their hymnbooks and Bibles—the books they have learned to read.

36

Composition Theme

The Rich Fool

Take heed, and beware of covetousness: for a man's life consisteth not in the abundance of the things which he possesseth.

And [Jesus] spake a parable unto them, saying, The ground of a certain rich man brought forth plentifully: and he thought within himself, saying, What shall I do, because I have no room where to bestow my fruits?

And he said, This will I do: I will pull down my barns, and build greater; and there will I bestow all my fruits and my goods. And I will say to my soul, Soul, thou hast much goods saved up for many years; take thine ease, eat, drink, and be merry.

But God said unto him, Thou fool, this night thy soul shall be required of thee: then whose shall those things be, which thou hast provided?

So is he that layeth up treasure for himself, and is not rich toward God.

LUKE 12:15–21

37

 Rebellion in the Hive

BY MARGARET GATTY

PART I

One lovely summer morning, a young bee (we shall call her a traveler bee) left her hive to gather nectar. The sun shone so brightly and the air felt so warm that she flew a long distance, till she came to some gardens that were bright with colorful flowers. There she roamed about, in and out of the flowers, buzzing in great delight, till she had so loaded herself with treasure that she could carry no more, and she thought of returning home.

But just as she was beginning her journey, she accidentally flew through the open window of a country house and found herself in a large dining room. There was a great deal of noise, for it was dinnertime, and the guests were talking rather loudly. As the bee was tasting some rich sweets in a dish on the table, she heard a child exclaim with a shout, "Oh, there's a bee! Let me catch it."

At this she rushed back, as she thought, to the open air. But, alas! In another second the poor thing found that she had flung himself against a hard, transparent wall. She had flown against one of the glass panes of the window—being quite unable, in her alarm and confusion, to distinguish the glass from the opening by which she had entered.

This unexpected blow annoyed her much. Having wearied herself in vain attempts to find the entrance, she began to walk slowly and quietly up and down the wooden frame at the bottom of the panes, hoping to recover both her strength and her composure.

Presently her attention was attracted by the soft, half-whispering voices of two children who were kneeling down and looking at her.

"This is a worker bee," said one. "I see the pollen bags under its thighs. How busy it has been! Yes, it's a worker bee—poor wretch!"

"Why do you call it 'poor wretch'?"

"Well, Uncle Collins says all people who work for other people and don't work for themselves are poor wretches. That is just what this bee does. There is the queen bee in the hive who does nothing at all but sit at home, give orders, and lay eggs; and all the bees wait upon her and obey her. Then there are the drones, lazy fellows who lounge all their time away. And there are the worker bees, like this one, who do all the work for everybody. How Uncle Collins would laugh at them if he knew!"

"Does Uncle Collins know about bees?"

"No, I think not. It was the gardener who told me. I heard Uncle Collins say another thing yesterday. He said that kings and queens are not right. Nature never makes one man a king and another a cobbler, but makes them all alike; and so, he says, kings and queens are very unjust things."

"Bees have not the sense to know anything about that," observed the girl.

"Of course not. Only fancy how angry these workers

would be if they knew what else the gardener told me!"

"What was that?"

"He said that the worker bees are just the same as the queen when they are first born. It is only the food that is given them and the shape of the house they live in that make the difference. The bee nurses manage that. They give some one sort of food, and some another, and they make the rest worker bees. It is just what Uncle Collins says about kings and cobblers: nature makes them all like. But look, dinner is over. We must go."

"Wait till I let the bee out," said the girl, gently taking up the traveler bee in a soft handkerchief.

"Poor thing!" she said. "So you might have been a queen if they had given you the right food and put you into the right-shaped house. What a shame they didn't! As it is, you must go and drudge away all your life long, making honey and wax. Well, get along with you! Return to your labors!"

Then she fluttered her handkerchief through the open window, and the bee found herself once more floating in the air.

PART II

It was a fine evening, but the traveler bee did not think so. She felt as if there were a dark, heavy cloud over the sky. Really, the cloud was over her own heart. She had become discontented and ambitious, and she rebelled at having to be a mere worker.

At last she reached her home, the hive that she had left with such a happy heart in the morning. After dashing in angrily, she began to unload the bags under her thighs; and as she did so, she exclaimed, "I am the most wretched of creatures!"

"What is the matter? What have you done?" cried an

old relation who was at work near her. "Have you been eating poisonous flowers, or have you discovered that the mischievous honey moth has laid her eggs in our combs?"

"Oh, neither, neither!" answered the bee impatiently. "But I have traveled a long way, and have heard a great deal about myself that I never knew before, and I know now that we are a set of wretched creatures."

"And pray, what wise animal has been teaching you that?" asked the old relation.

"I have learned a truth," answered the bee, "and it matters not who taught it to me."

"Certainly not; but you should not fancy yourself wretched merely because some foolish creature has told you that you are. You know very well that you were never wretched till you were told you were. I call that very silly; but I shall say no more to you."

The old relation then turned herself round to her work, singing very pleasantly all the time.

But the traveler bee would not be laughed out of her wretchedness. She collected some of her young companions round her and told them what she had heard in the large dining room of the country house. All were astonished, and most were vexed. The bee was so much pleased at causing such excitement and interest that she became sillier every minute, and made a long speech. She declared that there ought to be no such things as queens, and talked of all bees being equal and alike. The angry way she talked would have delighted Uncle Collins himself.

When the bee had finished her speech, there was first a silence, then a few buzzes of anger, and then much planning and wishing. Some wished Uncle Collins would come and manage all the beehives in the country, for they were sure he would let all the bees be queens, and then what a jolly time they would have!

Just then the old relation popped her head around the corner of the cell she was building.

"What would be the fun of being queens," she asked, "if there were no worker bees to wait on one?"

But the rebels buzzed very loudly and told her she was a fool. They said Uncle Collins would take care that the tyrant queen, and the royal children in their nurse cells, should wait on them while they lasted.

"And when they are finished?" persisted the old relation with a laugh.

"Buzz, buzz," was the answer; and the old relation held her tongue.

Then another bee suggested that after all, it would be very awkward for them all to be queens. Who would make the honey and wax, and build the honeycombs, and nurse the children? Would it not be best, therefore, that there should be no queens whatever, but that they should all be worker bees?

But then the tiresome old relation popped her head around the corner again and said she did not quite see how that change would benefit them, for were they not all worker bees already? At this there was such an indignant buzz that she retreated again to her work.

Night at last came on; the labors of the day were over, and sleep and silence reigned in the hive. But with the dawn, troubled thoughts returned. The traveler bee and her companions kept clustering together in little groups to talk over their wrongs and a remedy. Meantime, the rest of the hive were too busy to pay much attention to them, and so their idleness was not detected.

At last a few hotheaded youngsters grew so violent that a noisy quarrel would have broken out, but the traveler bee flew to them and suggested that as they were grown up now, and could not all be turned into queens, they had best sally forth and try the experiment of all being worker bees without any queen whatever. With this idea in view, she easily persuaded them to join her; and a very nice swarm they looked as they emerged into the open air and dispersed about the garden to enjoy the early breeze.

But a swarm of bees without a queen to lead them proved to be only a helpless crowd after all. The first thing they attempted was to decide on a home.

"A garden, of course," said one.

"A field," said another.

"There is nothing like a hollow tree," remarked a third.

"The roof of a good shed is the best protection from wet," thought a fourth.

"The branch of a tree will give us the most liberty," cried a fifth.

"I won't give up to anybody!" shouted all.

"I am very angry with you!" cried the traveler bee at last. "Half the morning is gone already, and here we are, as unsettled as when we left the hive."

"One would think you were to be queen over us, to hear you talk!" exclaimed the others. "If we choose to spend our time in quarreling, what is that to you? Go and do as you please!"

She did. She was ashamed and unhappy, and flew to the end of the garden to hide her vexation. There, seeing a clump of beautiful jonquils, she dived into a flower to soothe herself by gathering nectar. How she enjoyed it! She loved the flowers and their nectar more than ever, and began her accustomed murmur of delight. She had serious thoughts of going back at once to the hive as usual, and was just coming out of one of the golden cups when she met the old relation coming out of another.

"Who would have thought to find you here alone?" asked the old relation. "Where are your companions?"

"I scarcely know. I left them outside the garden."

"What are they doing?

"Quarreling," murmured the traveler bee.

"What about?"

"What they are to do."

"What a pleasant occupation for bees on a sunshiny morning!" said the old relation.

"Don't laugh at me. Tell me what to do," said the puzzled traveler. "What Uncle Collins says about nature and our all being alike sounds very true, and yet somehow we do nothing but quarrel when we try to be all alike and equal."

"How old are you?" asked the old relation.

"A few weeks," answered the traveler.

"And how old am I?"

"Many months, I am afraid."

"You are right, I am an oldish bee. Well then, friend, let us fight."

"Not for the world. I am the stronger and would hurt you."

"I wonder what makes you ask advice of a creature so much weaker than yourself."

"What has weakness to do with wisdom, my good old relation? I consult you because I know you are wise, and I am humbled, and feel that I am foolish."

"Old and young—strong and weak—wise and foolish! What has become of our being alike and equal? But never mind, we can manage. Now let us agree to live together."

"With all my heart. But where shall we live?"

"Tell me first which of us is to decide, if we differ."

"You shall. You are wise."

"Good! And who shall collect honey for food?

"I will. I am strong."

"Very well; you have made me a queen and yourself a worker bee! Ah, my foolish friend! Won't the old home and the old queen do? Don't you see that if even no more than two people live together, there must be a head to lead and hands to follow? How much more in the case of a multitude!"

Glad was the song of the traveler bee as she wheeled over the flowers, joyously agreeing with what she had heard.

"I will find my companions!" she cried at last, and the two flew away together and sought the knot of discontented youngsters outside the garden wall.

They were still quarreling, but with little energy. They were hungry and confused, and many had flown away to work and go home as usual.

Very soon afterward a cluster of happy buzzing bees, headed by the old relation and the traveler, returned with pollen-laden thighs to their hive. As they were about to enter, they were stopped by one of the little sentinels at the doorway.

"Wait!" she cried. "A dead young queen is passing out."

"How is this? What has happened?" asked the traveler bee. "Surely our queen is not dead?"

"Oh, no," answered the sentinel. "But something went wrong in the hive this morning. Some of the cell keepers were absent, and a young queen bee burst through. The two queens fought till one was dead, and the weaker one was killed. We shall not be able to send off a swarm quite so soon as usual this year; but these accidents can't be helped."

"But this one might have been helped," thought the traveler bee to herself.

"You see," buzzed the old relation, nudging her, "even queens are not equal! There can be but one ruler at once!"

"Yes," murmured the traveler bee.

38

 The Brickfields of Bristol

The following account has been adapted from the book *Horseman of the King,* by Cyril Davey. It takes place in England about the year 1739. In it we learn how John Wesley, who came to be known as the father of Methodism, first began to preach out-of-doors—having been banned from church pulpits in London for his fiery, Bible-centered messages.

PART I

"He's ridden a long way!" the stall owner declared, looking at the young man guiding his horse through the narrow street. It stumbled on the slimy cobblestones, and the rider almost slipped from the saddle.

"And ridden hard too, judging by the horse," answered the woman standing by him. She turned back to the tawdry articles displayed on the rough board. "Ah, well, parsons should be used to riding. They go fox hunting often enough."

"Just about the only thing most of them put their mind to, except eating and drinking with their rich neighbors." He took the small coin the woman handed him for the vegetables she had picked up. "Now if they were all like that parson Whitefield we've been hearing

165

so much about, and thought a bit more about helping
country folk like you and me, I might be more interested.
I might even go to church sometimes!"

"Ah, you might!" exclaimed the woman. "You might
indeed."

John Wesley rode on through the crowded lanes of

Bristol, past the old Dutch House and down the twisting
length of Wine Street. He had set out from London on
Thursday; now it was Saturday afternoon. A few minutes later he drew rein outside a little grocer's shop, not
far from the pillory and the whipping post. This was
George Whitefield's lodging.

It had been a stiff ride, and he had hardy noticed the
country he passed through. He had not really wanted to
come at all, and yet he could not stay in London. His
closest friends had angrily denounced George
Whitefield's open-air preaching as silly and wrong. They

urged him to refuse Whitefield's request asking John to join him in his work. At last, after John had prayed and fasted, he decided to go. Throughout the long ride, he had wondered if he was doing right. Even now that he had reached Bristol, he had decided only to see what was happening.

He hung his horse's reins over the post outside the grocer's shop and went in.

PART II ·

Late into the night Wesley and Whitefield talked. The two new friends found that they had much in common. Nevertheless, John insisted that he had come, not to take over George's work as George had requested, but simply to judge for himself whether outdoor evangelism was right. The next morning they were up at dawn, and John set out with an uneasy mind to share in one of the busiest Sundays he had ever known.

April sunshine broke through the clouds as he followed Whitefield to a grassy area on the outskirts of Bristol, where crowds of people had already gathered. John stood near his friend and watched the faces of people as they listened. It struck him that they were the same kind of people he had seen in the less well-to-do districts in London; people he had wanted to talk to; ordinary, poor, working people who were never found in church. Could it be, after all, that God was showing him the way?

From their first meeting place, they set out for Hanham Mount, at Kingswood. Once it had been a lovely, royal park. Now this wide area outside the city of Bristol was covered with slag heaps, huge piles of earth, and rubbish. It was dirty and depressing, and worse than that were the rows and rows of "houses" John saw wherever he looked. He supposed they were houses; certainly people lived in them. But as far as he could see, they were no more than square brick boxes, dirty outside and probably filthy inside. This was evident from the appearance of the children, who were thin, ill kempt, and dressed in rags.

As soon as they saw Whitefield, hundreds of these people surged toward him. Their sullen faces broke into smiles, and the children fought each other to get near him and hold his hand.

There was an even bigger crowd not far away at Rose Green, where George Whitefield preached for the third time that day. At each place, he told the people the same thing. He would have to leave Bristol because God had called him to preach again in America. When they asked what was to happen while he was away, he made the same reply at each place: "God, who calls me away, will send someone to take my place!"

Each time he said it, John avoided his glance. But he could not pretend to be deaf to his friend's entreating words as they walked home that afternoon.

And so, later that evening he found himself near the river that runs through the center of Bristol. He had agreed to go and talk to a little company of people who gathered in Nicholas Street. George Whitefield was not far away, at a similar meeting at a house in Baldwin Street.

There were few to listen to John, but the house where Whitefield was preaching was so filled with people that he could not even get upstairs and into the room. Instead, he had to climb to the roof of the house next door, scramble across the slippery tiles, and drop through a window into the room where his friends were waiting. This extraordinary beginning to the meeting, however, was not so important as its end.

George Whitefield looked around the room when the meeting was over. "My good friend John Wesley came from London yesterday," he announced. "He has been with me to Kingswood today. He will preach in the brickyard at the end of St. Philip's Fields tomorrow morning."

Back in their rooms, he told John what he had promised; and before dawn, Whitefield was riding to Gloucester on the way to London. John had not agreed to help, but after prayerful consideration, he decided to preach in the morning as Whitefield had done—just once. Perhaps, little as he wanted to do it, God would use this occasion to speak to him. He set out for the brickfields.

To his astonishment, more people were there than had been at any of the meetings to listen to Whitefield the day before. He looked around at their eager, curious faces. There were no hymns, no prayers. He could only speak to them as he had seen George do. He breathed a prayer for God's help and climbed onto a little mound. There was a deep silence.

"I have come to you in the Name of Jesus. He too spoke to the people in the fields. At the very beginning, Jesus told them why He had come. 'The Spirit of the Lord is upon me, because he hath anointed me to preach the gospel to the poor. . . .' " Nearly three thousand people listened to the clear, well-pitched voice. Many broke into tears as John spoke of God's love for them. Others came and stood on the outskirts of the crowd or sat on the clay banks.

"Mr. Whitefield was right," more than one man said to his neighbors when it was over. "God had taken him away—and sent a greater man in his place!"

By the time the meeting was over, John knew that what he had done was right. God wanted him to bring the message of Jesus to the fields and villages and town squares of England. What had begun in the brickfields, John knew in his heart, he would never be able to stop.

39

God Is Love

God is love, His mercy brightens
    All the path in which we move;
Bliss He forms, and woe He lightens;
    God is light, and God is love.

Chance and change are busy ever;
    Worlds decay, and ages move;
But His mercy waneth never;
    God is light, and God is love.

E'en the hour that darkest seemeth
    Will His changeless goodness prove;
From the mist His brightness streameth;
    God is light, and God is love.

He with earthly cares entwineth
    Hope and comfort from above;
Ev'rywhere His glory shineth;
    God is light, and God is love.

JOHN BOWRING

40

 The Lost Boy

AUTHOR UNKNOWN

Late in the summer of 1816, I was on a visit in a remote seaside village in Maine. The house where I was staying was about a stone's throw from the water and was owned by a family that I had known for many years. It consisted at that time of Mr. Mason, his wife, and their son Charles, who was about eight years of age. The event which occurred during my stay with them, I shall never forget. The distress it caused the parents and the excitement it caused the village have fixed it too deeply in my memory.

About a quarter of a mile from Mr. Mason's cottage was a small cove, which the few fishermen who lived in the village used as a harbor for their boats. At the time of this story, most of the fishermen were at sea, and a single sloop with a few small skiffs were the only boats in the harbor.

Mr. Mason had often told his son to avoid the boats, and on no account to venture into them alone or with his schoolfellows; but only with his father's permission and under the care of someone he could trust.

This particular afternoon in August, Charles Mason was idling along the seashore, skimming pebbles over the water and wishing he could swim. At length he reached the quiet harbor and saw a little boat tied to a stake in the bank. Without thinking a moment of his father's commands, he jumped into the boat and began paddling it about with a broken oar that he found in its bottom.

After he had been playing for some time, passing to and fro within a dozen yards of the land, he began, in spite of all his efforts, to be carried farther and farther from the shore. The tide had changed and was carrying the little boat swiftly along with it.

Charles was a brave boy and not to be frightened easily. He lay down calmly in the boat, expecting at the change of tide to be carried back in the same manner as he was being borne away. In almost no time, the little boat was carried beyond the harbor mouth and into a large bay. The bay was five or six miles across and dotted here and there with little islands three or four acres in size. As he was carried long, Charles hoped that he would be cast upon one of these islands; but one after another they passed, and he was still on the water. Nevertheless, it was some hours to sunset, and the little boy kept up his courage.

The last island in the bay was about ten miles from the mainland. Charles patiently waited to see if he should be landed there. The boat touched at last on the tip of a jutting point, and Charles leaped ashore.

The island on which he landed was quite large. It was lined with rocks and covered by a small woods and a few straggling whortleberry bushes. Charles pulled the boat ashore as best he could and then left it, intending to run about till the tide changed. He strayed some distance from the boat, however, and the sun went down while he was trying in vain to find his way back again.

Meanwhile, concern was mounting at home because of his absence. Hour after hour passed, and still Charles did not return. His parents grew alarmed and began to search for him. He had not been seen during the whole afternoon by any of his usual playmates. No trace of him could be found.

The villagers issued forth in search of the missing child. Men and women, young and old, explored every part of the neighborhood. The whole village was in motion. Lanterns were glancing from hill and valley and along the rocky shoreline of the little cove, until the gray of the morning made them unnecessary.

The search continued with unabated vigor until noon of the following day. It was then supposed that Charles had fallen into one of the lakes or ponds in the area. All were dragged or drained to no avail. It was impossible to find any clue to his fate. The distress of his mother was deeper than language can tell. I have never seen such anguish. She had given up all hope and would not be comforted.

Four days had now passed since the boy's disappearance, and the search was at a standstill. On the afternoon of the fourth day, a home-bound fishing vessel picked up the boat in which Charles had been carried away. The returning tide had swept the boat from the bank where he had fastened it.

The boat had not been missed earlier; but it was immediately believed to have some connection with Charles' disappearance. This revived a slight hope. It was possible that Charles might have been saved on one of the islands!

Early the next morning, all the men and boats that could be mustered were engaged in visiting the islands in the bay. The nearest ones were searched, but no trace of the child was found. The largest and most distant, however, remained unvisited. The weather had come in very stormy and lowering, and it finally became dangerous for small craft to be on the water. Most of the boats were forced to put back. Mr. Mason and I were in the only boat that remained at sea. We were determined to persevere at whatever hazard while there was any chance of finding Charles.

With a good deal of difficulty, we succeeded in reaching the most distant island. We examined it from one end to the other, shouting at every pace to attract the notice of the child; but it was all in vain. We gave up the search as hopeless.

As the storm had by this time abated, we entered our boat and put off, tired and distressed. We had not traveled twice the boat's length, however, when on turning to cast a final glance toward the island, I saw, on top of a rock about twenty yards from the beach, the weak and emaciated figure of Charles.

We found him entirely exhausted from fatigue, want of food and water, and fear. For five days he had lived on the few wild berries that he found on the island. He had heard our shouts but in his weakness had been unable to answer them. He had just enough strength to raise himself upon the rock where he lay; and when we reached him, he fainted in our arms.

Charles recovered in a short time. His mother, however, was thrown into a fever by her distress over his loss and by the violence of her joy at his unexpected return. Much time was to pass before events in the home of Charles Mason were to return to normal.

How much sorrow and suffering, reader, may spring from one act of thoughtless disobedience!

41

 The Beautiful Home

BY MARY R. Z. MILLER

"Look at that house!" Lois exclaimed. "Oh, isn't it beautiful?"

"Yes, it is," her mother agreed. "It *might* be nice to work there. On the other hand, we must keep in mind that outward appearances can be deceiving."

Lois kept her eyes focused on the beautiful house, the nicely trimmed trees, and the well-kept lawn. Numerous flower beds completed the picturesque setting. The car sped on, leaving this scene of loveliness behind.

"Oh, I surely would enjoy working in such a beautiful place," Lois sighed, dropping back against the seat.

"I wonder if it will be hard to find work in this community," Lois mused. It had been easy to find jobs back in Pleasantville. There were many working mothers there who needed someone to care for their children. The jobs were more plentiful than maids, so she had been able to be pretty choosy about where she worked.

"But it will be different here, I am sure," Lois thought. "It is such a small community with no big cities near. Most of the folks here are farmers, it seems. I

175

doubt if many of the women are working away or hiring maids. But that house has a different look. It doesn't fit into this community. Perhaps the woman who lives there might hire a maid for a day or two a week. I hope so." Lois allowed her thoughts to continue dreamily. "By all appearances, it would be a lovely place to work. I imagine it has the most modern conveniences, and of course, a happy mistress, thankful to own all that loveliness." By this time Lois had entirely forgotten her mother's words about judging by appearances.

Now they were passing a large, run-down, two-story house. The barn and sheds looked as if they had outlived their purpose many years ago. Apparently someone lived there who did not care how things looked. "Maybe they don't appreciate their things enough to care," Lois thought. "Or perhaps they are older people and are no longer able to keep things tidy. I am glad that type of people doesn't often hire girls." Lois shuddered at the thought of working at that shabby-looking place. The lure of the brick house was indelibly stamped upon her mind.

Before long the car slowed to turn onto the long dirt road leading to the small farm that Lois's father had purchased.

Moving day soon came, followed by days of arranging and rearranging and getting settled. During this time Lois was far too busy to think about working out.

Then when life had almost returned to normal, a telephone call came. "Is there anyone at your house interested in doing day work?" a soft, shaky voice asked.

"Yes," Lois answered. "I may be. Who is calling, please?"

"Mrs. Olen," said the voice at the other end of the line. "And what is your name?"

"I am Lois. Do you live nearby, Mrs. Olen?"

"Yes, we are the last two-story house before you turn in to your farm."

Lois's heart sank. The shabby, old, two-story house. She took a deep breath. "What did you want done, Mrs. Olen?"

"My husband and I are getting old. We live here alone. I would just like to have someone come and help me clean the house on Fridays. Could you come this week?"

Lois hesitated. She did want a job, but the thought of working in that gloomy old house was not appealing. Finally she said "Yes, Mrs. Olen, I'll come if it's all right with my parents. I'll let you know immediately if anything changes." With the arrangements made, Lois hung up the phone.

"Oh, why couldn't it be the beautiful brick house down the road?" she sighed. "Well, at least I have a job. I am thankful for that." Lois spent most of the remainder of the day thinking about the old house. "There will probably be high, dusty ceilings; a dirty old fireplace; black, worn linoleum; and maybe a grouchy old lady." Wistfully, Lois's thoughts returned to the beautiful brick house.

That evening the telephone rang again. "Well, it is a good thing we had a telephone installed right away," Lois laughed, walking toward the kitchen. "We haven't been here two weeks yet! How did we become so popular so fast?"

"Hello."

"Yes, I may be available for work," she answered the snappy little voice on the other end of the line. "Who is calling, please?"

The snappy voice continued.

"And where do you live, Mrs. Ray?"

A smile came over Lois's face. "Yes, I know where that is. . . . No, I'm sorry, I would not be able to help you on

Friday. I'm already engaged for that day. . . . Yes, I would be glad to come tomorrow morning. . . . Good-bye. . . ."

"Mother," Lois called excitedly. "Guess what! That was the lady from that beautiful brick house! You remember the one we were admiring? And she wants me to clean for her. Now I have a job for Thursdays and Fridays. I can hardly wait to see inside her home."

The next morning, Lois eagerly prepared to go to work and soon pulled up to the lovely brick house. "James T. Ray." Lois read aloud the sign on the mailbox. "This is it," she thought. "Oh, I am sure I will enjoy working here. Everything is so lovely!"

"Good morning, Mrs. Ray," Lois spoke cheerily when the door opened to her knock. She stood before a small, wiry, tight-featured woman still in her housecoat.

"Good morning," Mrs. Ray returned dryly, looking as if she thought it was anything but good. Just then her husband appeared, asking where his green shirt was.

"In the ironing basket," she snapped, not turning her eyes from their close scrutiny of Lois.

"You knew I wanted that shirt today," Mr. Ray growled in the background as he strode down the carpeted hall.

"Wear the one you wore yesterday!" Mrs. Ray shouted after him.

Lois felt embarrassed. She followed Mrs. Ray into the house.

"That man!" Mrs. Ray hissed. "He's never satisfied. He knows I have a headache this morning, but he hollers at me anyway. I was so busy all day yesterday that I could not get that shirt ironed. Well, here," she broke off suddenly, changing the subject. "You clean this kitchen. I'll go and set up the ironing board for you."

In the quietness of the sparkling white kitchen, Lois was left alone with her thoughts. There were only a few dishes. "I hope Mrs. Ray doesn't often get up with a headache. She might be a little more pleasant if she felt well." Before long, Lois noticed a third plate on the breakfast table and decided there must be one other member in the household. She hoped it would be a child or someone she could talk to. She could hear Mr. and Mrs. Ray arguing in an adjoining room. "How can I stand it here all day if Mr. and Mrs. Ray continue their arguing?" she wondered.

It took only a short while for Lois to finish in the kitchen. Next would be the ironing. Drying her hands on her apron, she stepped into the spacious and exquisitely furnished front room.

"Don't drip that on that rug!" Mrs. Ray screamed.

Startled, Lois looked at her hands and then at Mrs. Ray.

"I wasn't talking to you," Mrs. Ray explained, half apologetically.

It was then that Lois noticed a very small girl with a big bottle of Pepsi sitting in one corner of the room.

"Hello." Lois smiled in the awkward silence. "What is your name?"

"Marianna," the little girl replied. "I started to school last year. Now I'm in the second grade. I'm seven."

Lois was delighted.

"Now stop talking so much. She didn't ask for your life story. Go to the kitchen to drink that," Mrs. Ray ordered the child impatiently.

Before long, Mr. Ray left for work. Mrs. Ray showed Lois what needed to be ironed and then went into her bedroom. Marianna returned to the front room and climbed onto the sofa in front of the ironing board. From there, she keep a steady stream of chatter flowing.

"I don't know why Mother always screams at me," she began. "I wouldn't spill anything on her new rug.

But she worries all the time. She yells at Father too. We might mess up her pretty house. Father is nice if he doesn't get drunk. But he does. Sometimes he doesn't even come home. Then Mother is really mad."

Lois did not know what to say. How could she get this child to change the subject? Apparently she intended to thoroughly acquaint Lois with the Ray family before the day was over.

Soon Mrs. Ray reappeared and hurried Marianna out to wait for the school bus, much against the little girl's will. She was reluctant to be deprived of Lois's company.

"Hang the clothes here on this rod as you iron them. I'll show you where to put them later," Mrs. Ray said, opening the door to a small closet beside the ironing board.

After ironing for about two hours, Lois set down the iron and walked into the kitchen. "Mrs. Ray, I think I've hung about as many clothes on that rod as it will hold. Should I put some of them away before I iron the rest?"

"No," Mrs. Ray answered, lifting her head from the table. "Go and finish. Then we will put them away."

Slowly Lois turned and walked back to the front room. "Mrs. Ray looks as if she has been crying," Lois thought sympathetically. "She surely seems to be an unhappy woman."

"I'm sure this rod will not hold many more pieces," Lois worried, examining the shaky rod. "I don't know what is holding it up now." Carefully she hung several more shirts, but finally she put on one piece too many. The crash brought Mrs. Ray flying into the front room.

"What is going on?" she cried. Seeing the freshly ironed clothes in a heap on the floor, she lamented, "You should have known better than to put more on the rod than it would hold. Now you would hardly know they were ironed." Then her tone became sharp. "Just put them away! We don't have the time to do them all over again!"

Lois stood silently, waiting till the outburst was over. There were things she could have said, but she decided not to.

The day wore slowly on. As Lois was polishing the silverware, Mrs. Ray came to the kitchen to start supper. She was trying to open a jar of jelly when her husband came in. He walked past without a word, scarcely noticing her.

"See, he won't help me. He does not love me. He never offers a helping hand when he sees I cannot do something," Mrs. Ray complained. Her mood had not changed through the entire day.

Lois was glad when evening finally came. She thought as she got into her car to leave that neither the house nor the yard seemed quite as lovely, now that she knew what kind of home this really was.

Lois went to bed early that night, wondering what the next day at the old house would be like.

The morning dawned bright and clear, and it seemed to Lois, when she arrived at the old house, that the early sun cast away much of its weather-beaten look.

"Good morning, Lois." An elderly Mrs. Olen was beaming from the open door. "Come in. I am glad to meet you."

"Good morning," Lois returned cheerfully, stepping into the Olens' cozy, inviting kitchen. It had high ceilings, a gray board floor, and colorful but faded walls. Beside a large wood cookstove sat an elderly man holding a rough, well-worn cane. An old black dog lay curled at his feet.

"Lois, this is my husband," Mrs. Olen introduced the old man, lovingly patting his shoulder. "He is my eyes and I am his feet. I don't see so well, you know, but I can still get around fairly well. His feet have traveled about as far as they will go, but he helps me with his eyes." At this, Mr. Olen smiled and nodded his head; then he reached down and gave his dog a scratch.

Lois felt perfectly at ease all day as she worked with Mrs. Olen. There was such a comfortable, homelike atmosphere in the old house. It was refreshing to see how the dear old couple loved each other.

"We have lived together for more than sixty years now," Mrs. Olen chatted pleasantly. "God has been good to us. We have always had all we needed—enough to make us happy but not so much that it makes us discontented. We do not have a thing to complain about. Why, it would take us from now till the day we die to thank the Lord for all that He has already done for us."

Lois continued scrubbing floors while Mrs. Olen dusted the crude, homemade table and old, wooden rocking chairs. In her mind, she was comparing two homes—a beautiful home and a very plain one.

"Our things aren't fancy," the contented little lady continued, "but they are comfortable, and we still have each other—that is more than most people can say at our age." She continued to count her blessings while Mr. Olen sat by the kitchen stove, shelling pecans for her cake.

Week after week, as Lois continued to go to these two homes, she became more and more conscious of the warmth and beauty of the one—and the poverty of the other.

42

The Plough

Above yon sombre swell of land
   Thou seest the dawn's grave orange hue,
With one pale streak like yellow sand,
   And over that a vein of blue.

The air is cold above the woods
   All silent is the earth and sky;
Except with his own lonely moods
   The blackbird holds a colloquy.

Over the broad hill creeps a beam,
   Like hope that gilds a good man's brow;
And now ascends the nostril steam
   Of stalwart horses come to plough.

Ye rigid ploughmen, bear in mind
   Your labour is for future hours;
Advance—spare not—nor look behind—
Plough deep and straight with all your powers!

RICHARD HENRY HORNE

43

 The Laborers
in the Vineyard

MATTHEW 20:1–16

For the kingdom of heaven is like unto a man that is an householder, which went out early in the morning to hire labourers into his vineyard. And when he had agreed with the labourers for a penny a day, he sent them into his vineyard.

And he went out about the third hour, and saw others standing idle in the marketplace, and said unto them, "Go ye also into the vineyard, and whatsoever is right I will give you." And they went their way.

Again he went out about the sixth and ninth hour, and did likewise.

And about the eleventh hour he went out, and found others standing idle, and saith unto them, "Why stand ye here all the day idle?"

They say unto him, "Because no man hath hired us."

He saith unto then, "Go ye also into the vineyard; and whatsoever is right, that shall ye receive."

So when even was come, the lord of the vineyard saith unto his steward, "Call the labourers, and give them their hire, beginning from the last unto the first."

And when they came that were hired about the eleventh hour, they received every man a penny. But when the first came, they supposed that they should have received more; and they likewise received every man a penny.

And when they had received it, they murmured against the goodman of the house, saying, "These last have wrought but one hour, and thou hast made them equal unto us, which have borne the burden and heat of the day."

But he answered one of them, and said, "Friend, I do thee no wrong: didst not thou agree with me for a penny? Take that thine is, and go thy way: I will give unto this last, even as unto thee. Is it not lawful for me to do what I will with mine own? Is thine eye evil, because I am good?"

So the last shall be first, and the first last: for many be called, but few chosen.

44

 The Basketmaker of Cavan

ADAPTED FROM A TRUE STORY WRITTEN
BY SARAH T. WAYLAND IN 1849

PART I

Many years ago, in the county of Cavan, Ireland, there lived an elderly lady who was known far and wide for her deeds of kindness. Mrs. Farnham was her name, and she had enough money that she could have lived in pleasure. But knowing that "she that liveth in pleasure is dead while she liveth," she had chosen rather to live a plain and quiet life.

Near this lady lived a family so poor that they were considered hopeless by many. Their oldest boy, fifteen-year-old Ned, met Mrs. Farnham one morning near her house and begged for something for his family to eat. Mrs. Farnham stopped, and looking at him, she said, "My boy, I would like you to do something to earn your bread. Make me a basket. As soon as you have finished, bring it to me, and I will pay you well for it."

Ned liked the idea of earning what before he had received by begging. Ever since his father had died, Ned had been responsible for supplying his family's needs.

186

He was young, however, and people thought him undependable; so Ned had to beg for a livelihood. "This lady," thought Ned, "will pay me if I am willing to work. I never did make a basket, but I shall try," he resolved.

Ned went home and started working on his basket right away. He encountered many difficulties (for he had no one to teach him), and though sometimes rather perplexed, he was never completely discouraged. He kept on working until finally he had made a basket. With a happy heart, Ned ran to Mrs. Farnham's house and knocked loudly on the door.

Mrs. Farnham's housekeeper, who was not as charitable as Mrs. Farnham, opened the door.

"Mrs. Farnham asked me for a basket," Ned said timidly.

"Well, I am glad Mrs. Farnham is not home," snapped the housekeeper. "She is so kindhearted she likely would have taken the basket, even though she could buy nicer ones in town. No, my boy, we don't need your basket," and with that she closed the door. As Ned stood outside the house, tears came to his eyes; he thought his hope was gone.

Ned turned to leave, but then he noticed Mrs. Farnham and her son Clarence (who was much older than Ned) coming up the walk toward him. Ned looked at his basket, then at Mrs. Farnham, and hope again lit up his face.

She did not recognize Ned at first, but when she saw the basket, she said, "My good boy, so you have my basket! And for a first basket it's a very nice one, isn't it, Clarence?" She pressed a piece of money into his hand and said, "Go on and make more baskets, and I will help you sell them."

Ned's happy smile more than repaid her for the kindness she had shown.

Clarence looked at Ned's old, worn clothes as the boy sped off with his wages. "I wish, Mother," he said, "that I could give Ned some of my clothes. His are in such poor condition."

"If Ned is willing to work," his mother replied, "I think he will soon be able to buy clothes for himself."

This incident was a turning point in Ned's life. Until then, he had never earned a penny or known the pleasure of hard work. He felt something like self-respect as he hurried home, resolving to spend his money wisely and to make the best baskets that he was able.

He worked hard, and in a few days he had two more baskets completed—both a good deal better than the first. These won an approving smile from Mrs. Farnham, and she introduced him to men who were willing to buy all the baskets Ned could deliver.

Ned went on improving his baskets. In a few short years, they were among the best to be found in Cavan. Others of his family were drawn into the business until after a time the family was in no great need. And all knew that it was largely because of Ned's hard work and perseverance.

PART II

Though Ned was hard-working, he found time to read the Bible that Mrs. Farnham had given him. Also, he began to attend services at the church she attended.

Ned loved to hear the hymns of faith and especially two which he knew to be favorites of Mrs. Farnham. Although they were written in French (which was Mrs. Farnham's native language), Ned soon became so familiar with these two songs that he resolved to translate them into Gaelic, his native Irish tongue.

Over the past few years, Ned had developed a conversational knowledge of the French of Mrs. Farnham, but he soon found that to translate the songs was a very difficult matter. The difficulties were even greater than his first efforts at basketmaking. However, he persevered, and finally the two songs were translated. These songs Ned's family learned to sing together.

"Clarence, I have been looking for some way to repay your mother for her kindness to me," Ned told Clarence when the two met one day. "I have heard that she has been sick, and I was wondering if our family could come to your house to sing for her."

"I think Mother would like that very much, Ned," replied Clarence. "Why don't you come over this evening?"

Ned was delighted at the prospect of singing for Mrs. Farnham, and he returned to his home humming the tunes he had worked on for so long.

"Mother," said Clarence that evening, "I have picked some flowers and put them in a vase on the sitting room table. Would you like to go there? I think it would do you good to sit up for a while."

"It has been more than a week since I have been in the sitting room," Mrs. Farnham replied. "Yes, I would like to go there and see your flowers."

When she was seated, Mrs. Farnham commented on the beauty of the bouquet and then requested that Clarence read some passages from the Bible. To this Clarence cheerfully complied, but soon his mother's attention was drawn to the sound of singing coming through an open window. The song she could hear was a favorite of hers, but the words were Irish.

"Clarence," she said, "who can this be?"

"It is Ned and his family," Clarence replied. "Ned has translated the song himself and has taught it to his family."

There were tears in Mrs. Farnham's eyes and a smile on her face as Clarence continued. "Ned is to be admired for the quiet way he works. We will never know the amount of effort that went into these translations."

"Clarence, please go immediately and invite Ned and his family in," said Mrs. Farnham. "I want to thank them for coming." After she had thanked each one of them, she turned again to Ned. "I want to encourage you in the work of translation. The Irish need more hymns in their own language."

Ned left with a brighter anticipation of the future than had before been his. He still enjoyed making baskets. But he now realized that the spiritual needs of his countrymen were more important than making baskets. So he spent more and more of his time in translating songs until after a number of years a book was printed of the songs which he had translated.

Ned, or shall be call him Mr. ———, had a daughter who inherited her father's love for singing. This talent she never displayed in public, but by the bedsides of invalids and children. Cavan became a delightful place to visit for anyone who loved the Lord. There one could clearly see what God can do with willing hands and seeking souls.

Such is the history of Ned the Basketmaker, a name of which he was never ashamed. Although it is a story of long ago, there were for many years those who remembered Ned and Mrs. Farnham. Diligence and perseverance and the grace of our Lord had raised Ned from a life of ignorance and poverty to an abundant life in Jesus Christ.

45

Charley and Anna

Charley

"Oh, summer is coming and now I can run!"
Said Charley one morn as he saw the bright sun.
"I'll run in the fields and hear the birds sing,
And I'll sing myself, till the forest shall ring.
I'll hunt up my kite and let it soar high,
And watch it, a speck floating up in the sky.
My hoe, and my cart that is painted so red,
I'll take to my garden and make a fine bed.
I will plant watermelon and green citron seeds,
For this year, I am sure, I shall keep out the weeds.
"I'll go to the pond and haul up my boat,
And get William to make it all ready to float;
We will sail 'cross the pond on the first day of May,
And gather sweet flowers that grow round the bay."

Anna

"But stop, little brother! Aren't you going too fast?
Such castles of pleasure perhaps will not last.
Though we say that *we will*, we don't always succeed;
And to be quite so certain is hazard indeed;

191

And whether it's work we engage in, or play,
We should look to our Father to prosper the way.
He provides for our wants, and in kindness will lead,
And permits or prevents as He thinks we best need."

AUTHOR UNKNOWN

46

Fifteen-barge Tow

BY D. GOOD

In this story we will discover how barges are pushed down the Ohio and Mississippi rivers to the deep sea harbor at New Orleans in the state of Louisiana. Our story begins with a towboat making up a tow on the Ohio River near the city of Cincinnati, Ohio.

PART I

"All hands on deck," the loudspeaker blares.

Two deck hands work feverishly to loosen the ropes that hold the *Cairo Monarch* snubbed against the dock. "All clear," they signal the pilot as they run forward to the bow of the towboat.

Three stories above, the *Monarch's* pilot casts a concerned look at the low-water marks on the dock. He smoothly moves the control lever forward, bringing six thousand horsepower to his command, and the 160-foot-long towboat surges ahead. With his other hand, the pilot moves the steering lever back and forth, maneuvering his charge into the open channel of the Ohio River. He reaches for the intercom to the engine room below.

"How are we doing down there?"

"Number one engine a little slow coming up to power. Number two, all right," the engineer replies.

"We are quite low in the channel," the pilot informs the engineer.

"Well, just so long as you keep the propellers off the bottom," the engineer returns.

"I'll do what I can," the pilot concludes with a chuckle as he sets himself to the task of making up a tow.

Ahead, a huge granary, filled with grain for overseas export, comes into view. Tied alongside it are five grain barges, riding like huge, floating train cars, one behind another against the dock. All but one have been filled. On the remaining barge, two men are directing a flexible downspout through which is flowing the last of an over-three-thousand-ton payload of grain. The loading completed, the shoreside crane operator swings the last hatch cover into place.

A dull thud vibrates the *Monarch* as she makes contact with the rearmost barge. Deck hands proceed to snub the barges to the "towing knees"; these are large steel-plated uprights at the front of the towboat which are used to push the tow. The *click-click* of ratchets sounds as the men tighten cables to lash the line of barges securely ahead of the towboat. Tied together, barge on barge, and in turn lashed to the towing knees of the *Monarch*, the unit that they form looks and acts like a single vessel. The term *towboat* is something of a misnomer, since the barges are pushed rather than pulled.

Other deck hands spill from the *Monarch* onto the barges and dash the 195 feet to the end of the first barge. One stays there as the others continue another 195 feet, where a second deck hand stations himself. This procedure continues until one man is on the bow of each barge, with the final man nearly a thousand feet ahead of the towboat.

The mate, equipped with a two-way radio, takes his place on one of the barges to direct the work of the deck hands.

"Let loose," the pilot's voice crackles over the mate's radio.

"Cut her loose," the mate relays the command to the deck hands.

Each man works his way back toward the towboat, loosening the ropes that hold the barges against the granary dock.

The mate presses the transmit button and says, "All clear." With a surge of power, the *Monarch* moves the grain barges into the channel.

Tied along a pier a short distance downriver are five more barges; these are filled with coal, bound for the eastern seaboard. They are open-hopper barges, much the same as the grain barges but without hatch covers.

Ropes fly through the air as the tow pulls up alongside them. Much like a cowboy bringing in a wild horse, the deck hands keep their snubbing ropes tight as the pilot backs, swings, and turns the *Monarch* to take on the additional barges. The tow now numbers ten barges.

The last five barges are brought alongside by another towboat. Of these barges, one has eight railroad cars piggybacked aboard, and another has five large grain combines lashed to the deck. The other three are tank barges holding petroleum products. The five newcomers are quickly lashed to the grain and coal barges, and the tow is complete.

"I want safety lines between all the barges," the pilot orders as he prepares to get under way.

PART II

The *Cairo Monarch,* with her fifteen-barge tow, moves into the channel to begin the 1,380-mile journey to New Orleans. "Full power ahead!" the pilot calls.

"Full power," the engineer returns.

"Do you think we will make the run in a week?" the pilot questions, as the *Monarch's* engines come up to full cruising speed.

"We have made it in six days," the engineer returns, "but with the water so low, we had better figure one or two days extra."

"Right, no speed records this round," the pilot agrees, turning his attention to a series of bridge piers in the channel ahead. Practiced hands turn the ship's wheel, and the barges and towboat pass through with only a few feet of clearance on either side.

Meanwhile, down in the galley the cook is feeding the off-watch crew. No sooner is the last dish served than a message comes over the intercom.

"All hands on deck for change of watch."

Conversation trails off as the men gulp down the last of their food and pour through the galley door to take their stations. "Like feeding two families," thinks the cook as he prepares for the crew that will soon fill his tables.

"Wind out of the southeast at fifteen knots requiring some constant left rudder. We should be coming up on the first lock in about an hour," the off-going pilot greets his counterpart.

"Roger! I'll radio for clearance," states the new pilot as he takes his place.

He radios ahead to the upcoming lock to make sure the upper gate is open and all is ready to "lock through" a fifteen-barge tow. Before long the lock gates come into view.

"Man the tow." The loudspeaker carries the pilot's command when the first of the barges near the lock.

Locks on the Ohio River system are needed to compensate for the natural drop in elevation along the river course. They are twelve hundred feet long, and only a single lockage is required at any one place.

Slowly the pilot eases the towboat and barges into the lock. The upper gate closes and the drain valve opens, allowing the water level to drop. Deck hands keep the tow snubbed against the lock wall to hold it steady as the water falls. Finally the lower gate opens, and the tow is on the way once again. Thus the procedure is established, and the *Monarch* and crew continue to log the river miles to New Orleans.

Two days of lockages and changing shifts pass before the tow reaches Cairo, Illinois, and the junction of the Ohio and the Mississippi rivers. Once on the winding Mississippi, the pilot is kept busy steering the tow around one S-curve after another. Samuel Clemens, a popular American writer, once described the shape of the Mississippi River like this: "If you will throw a long, pliant apple paring over your shoulder, it will pretty fairly shape itself into an average section of the Mississippi River; that is, the nine or ten hundred miles stretching from Cairo, Illinois, southward to New Orleans, the same being wonderfully crooked, with a brief straight bit here and there at wide intervals."

Night has fallen, and the pilot frequently peers into the radar viewer. Now he flips a switch, and a powerful searchlight breaks the darkness. With fingertip electronic controls, he directs the probing three-mile beam, searching for sandbars. Suddenly there is a terrible jar, and the pilot shifts quickly to full reverse.

"We are aground!" the mate radios from his station on one of the forward barges.

Powerful hydraulic rams push the rudders back and forth as the pilot tries to back the tow off the sandbar. Tired deck hands spill onto the deck in the excitement, eager to see what is happening.

"Man overboard!" The shout fills the night as the tow lurches off the sandbar and an unsuspecting deck hand tumbles into the water. The *Monarch's* engines are cut back to an idle, and the pilot swings a searchlight in the direction of the splashing crew member. Someone throws a lifesaving ring, and the deck hand is soon pulled on board. After graciously accepting the jests of his fellow workers, he heads toward the crew quarters for a change of clothes, then to the galley for some hot coffee.

Once clear of the sandbar, the pilot puts through a radiophone call to his superiors back in Cincinnati.

"How are things with the *Monarch*?" an official there asks.

"Slow at best," the pilot replies. "The water level is very low, and we've run aground once already. Figure on the ninth day for New Orleans."

And so the journey continues, with the kind of nerve-racking slowness that turns a pilot's hair gray.

Finally the tow reaches the New Orleans harbor, where tugboats relieve the *Monarch* of her tow and deliver the barges to where their contents can be transferred to ocean-going vessels. Thus cut loose, the towboat can take on another tow and start back up the Mississippi within a few hours. Once more she will contend with low water, winding rivers, sandbars, fog, and the numerous other challenges that arise in moving barges along America's eastern waterways.

47

 The Other Half
of the House

AUTHOR UNKNOWN

The four Mansueto children sat on the ladderlike steps of their side of the two-family house to watch the new neighbors moving into the other half of the house. Pedro, the two-year-old, sat on the top step where he could dodge quickly through the door to Mother and safety. Six-year-old Alicia's black, curly head was just below Pedro's small, bare feet. Pepita, who was eight, was brave enough to sit halfway down on step number six. Carlos, the big brother, sat only three steps from the ground, where he could protect the younger children and see the most. He had a good view, not only of the new neighbors' steps and yard and door, but also of the busy under-the-house space that is so useful in the rain-rich Philippians.

The new neighbors smiled at the four Mansuetos and tried to start a conversation while carrying mats, chairs, tables, kettles, dishes, and chests up the steps into their half of the house. But Carlos, Pepita, Alicia, and Pedro were too shy to answer—too shy even to smile. They just sat in a solemn row and stared with dark, wondering eyes.

The next day and the next, the children watched. Sometimes they watched from their steps, sometimes from the shade of the breadfruit tree in their half of the yard, and sometimes through the peek holes in the wall of woven palm fibers that separated their rooms from the rooms of their new neighbors.

The children knew everything that happened in the other half of the house. They knew when the boy and girl went to school, when the mother went to market, and when the father went off to talk with people.

Once or twice Carlos and Pepita followed the father and found that he talked with people on the street, or in the marketplace, or in homes. They heard him inviting people to come to his house the next Sunday morning. They thought he asked them to come to church in his house, but they knew they must not have understood. They knew that a church was a big building with a sad-faced statue in its yard and many images and candles in a big, dim room. The other half of the house was just like theirs—not a bit like a church.

The neighbors invited the Mansuetos for Sunday morning also. Father and Mother Mansuetos shook their heads while Pedro hid behind his mother, the little girls stared, and Carlos whispered a polite, "No, thank you, sir."

On the fourth day, Sunday, a strange thing happened in the half-house of the new neighbors. Just before nine o'clock in the morning, people began climbing up their steps. First came the owners of the variety store at the corner. Then came the schoolteacher and his family. Then came the grandmother of their friend Rosa, a man who drove a brown jeepney, the lady dentist with her three little girls, the man that worked in the drugstore, the potter who made clay pots and bowls, the cleaning woman from the big house with the star apple tree, a farmer who tied his carabao under the house, the boy who sold them little hard rolls for breakfast every morning, and a policeman in a clean, gray uniform.

The children began to wonder if the split-bamboo floor could hold so many people. Instead of worrying, however, they enjoyed the friendly talk coming from the open door and wide windows.

Suddenly the talking stopped. It was very still. Then the children heard one voice speaking slowly.

The little Mansuetos scrambled up their steps to join their parents, whose ears were close to the woven walls. They could hear every word in the other half of the house.

The voice stopped speaking. Someone hummed a tune. Then there was singing. At first it was hard to understand the words. Soon their ears grew used to the sounds. The Mansuetos heard the people singing about someone named Jesus. The words "We would see Jesus" came often. It was a good song. The little Mansuetos could hum it on their side of the thin wall while Mother kept time with her head and their father tapped his foot. There were other songs. Then they hear the voice again, the voice of the father of the new neighbors' family.

"We hope to have a church building of our own someday," he said. "Till then our church can meet here in our house."

In the weeks that followed, the peek holes in the woven walls grew larger from much use. There was one just the right height for Carlos, lower peek holes for each of his sisters, a very low one for little Pedro, and two high ones for their father and mother. The songs sung loudly on the other side of the wall were sung softly on the Mansuetos' side: "We Would See Jesus," "For the Beauty of the Earth," "Praise God From Whom All Blessings Flow." The sermons, prayers, and Bible readings came clearly through the thin walls. So did the stories told especially for children.

Finally one Sunday morning, Mother Mansueto dressed Alicia and Pepita in their newest and starchiest dresses. She told Carlos to scrub very clean at the cold faucet in the sink and to put on his best shirt and pants. The children could guess what was coming before she said, "You may go to the other side of the house this morning."

"You and Father will come with us? No?" asked Carlos.

"No." He will go to watch the cockfights soon, and I must stay here to take care of Pedro," said Mother.

Carlos reminded her, "Some children as small as Pedro will be there." He knew she was making excuses because she was afraid to go to anything but the large church in the city.

Three shy, clean children walked down the Mansueto steps and up their neighbors' steps that morning. They found the welcome and the happiness that a church always has for visitors or newcomers. The children had much to tell when they came back to their own half of the house.

They did not finish telling it that day. For five more days they were humming the songs, repeating the stories, and talking about next Sunday. Sometimes they heard their parents whispering together very seriously.

"What would the priest say?" the father would ask.

"He will never miss us," the mother would answer. "You know we never go to his church except on fiesta days when everybody goes."

"Let the children go a while longer," the parents agreed, "and see what happens."

So, Sunday after Sunday, the children went to church in the other side of the house. They went during the week too, for play and for classes. And all the time their parents saw them grow happier, kinder, more quick to obey.

Finally came the Sunday when Carlos, Alicia, and Pepita were not alone climbing down their steps and up their neighbors' steps. Mother Mansueto led Pedro with her. Father Mansueto grumbled a little about wasting time, but he went up the neighbors' steps too.

They must have liked what they found, because the whole family has been going to church ever since.

This true story happened on the Philippine island of Leyte almost twenty years ago. (The only part that is not true is the name of he family.) All but one of the Mansuetos sit in church pews every Sunday to hear the minister preach. One of them, Carlos, is in the pulpit of a church near Manila every Sunday.

The church where Carlos Mansueto preaches has a lovely building among the palms, with a porch and large window, pews with plenty of red-covered hymnbooks, and a pleasant room for Sunday school classes. Carlos is glad about all this, but he knows that it is not the building that makes a church. He will never forget how he peeked through a thin, woven wall into a room where a church with no building of its own was worshiping God.

48

 ## Composition Theme

"Lean Not Unto Thine Own Understanding"

Trust in the LORD with all thine heart; and lean not unto thine own understanding. In all thy ways acknowledge him, and he shall direct thy paths.

PROVERBS 3:5, 6

49

The Very School of Snow

BY H. W. BEECHER

The recent snowstorm brings back my boyhood experience. Reared among the hills of western Connecticut, I was brought up in the very school of snow. I remember the dreamy snowfalls, when great flakes came down wavering through the air as if they had no errand, and were sauntering for mere laziness.

The air thickens. One by one familiar objects are hidden as by a mist. Paths disappear. Voices of teamsters are heard, but no wagons can be seen in the road. Like a fog, the fast-falling snow hides all things. It comes straight down; not a breath of wind disturbs its descent. All day long it falls. The fences are grotesquely muffled; evergreens bend with their burden. Even the bare branches of deciduous trees are clothed as with wool.

Still the noiseless flakes fill the sky. The eye is bewildered in looking out upon the strange haze, so calm, so still, so full of movement, and yet with a sense of solitude in it!

But as you look, a change is taking place. The snowflakes are becoming smaller. They have lost their calm and leisurely motion. They begin to pelt down, as if shot by some force above. Now and then around the corner comes a puff of wind, which drives the snow off in long, slanting lines; or swirls of wind come, mixing them up in a strange medley.

Night is shutting in. Every moment the air darkens. The wind is coming in earnest. The chimney roars with a hollow and shuddering sound. There is no use looking out anymore; all is black. Drop the curtains. Throw on the logs. The flames fill the whole room with a warm glow. Draw round the table, for now there is a keen sense of home security.

The wind comes in gusts and smites the house till it groans, and at times you distinctly feel that it rocks under you. The blacker the night, the more turbulent the wind, the wilder the storm—all the more does each one within rejoice in the contrast. There is no such night at home in the country as a real stormy night.

But the young imagination is keen and summons all its treasures. It hears in the wind, voices of distress. Then come stories of wolves and benighted travelers. As the wind comes shrilly through cracks or keyholes, you start, as if a shriek sounded in your very ear. Now and then comes a buffet against the window, a straining and tugging at the side of the house, as if the night were seeking to storm the castle and break in all its defenses.

At length, one by one, the family members creep off to bed. You cuddle close together and pull the covers over your head to deaden the sound as well as to keep out the snow. For no double windows protected the old-fashioned house; the fine snow sifted in; and often the morning found scarfs of snow upon the bed.

But what a morning! The sun is up. The wind has gone down. The snow has ceased to fall but not to move. It is drifting in every direction. It hangs over the eaves.

It has buried the kitchen door. Fences are all gone. It is a new land. Yonder is the top of a haystack, and beyond it the roof of the shed. The barn yet towers up in sight. Woe to them who have no woodsheds and who now must dig out the unsheltered pile.

A way must be cut through the drift that buries the front door. Paths must be opened. Everyone in the neighborhood is busy. It will be several days before one village can communicate with another. For the roads are to be "broken out." The people turn out one and all. Men, boys, horses, all work with a will. Indeed, it is more like play than work.

Now then, you are ready for settled winter! Two or three feet of snow on a level, which will lie for two months! As soon as the snow hardens a little, you can take your own direction across the country.

Not a fence can be seen. Swamps can now be entered safely. The streams need no bridges. The woods are full of men getting out the year's fuel. Everyone is glad, while all the young people who love frolic are getting ready for sleigh rides. Winter in the country, to many, is the year's holiday.

50

 Cyrus McCormick
Invents the Reaper

BY ELIZABETH WATSON

This is the true story of a man named Cyrus Hall McCormick, who as a boy lived on a farm in the Shenandoah Valley in the beautiful Blue Ridge Mountains of Virginia.

At the time, being the beginning of the 1800s, almost everyone in the United States lived on a farm, and a great many of those farms were in the valleys along the rivers and streams that flowed to the sea. In those days there were only a few roads in the entire country, and those roads were so narrow, so rough, and so full of tree stumps and deep mud holes that people would not use them if they could possibly travel by water. Everyone tried to live near a river or stream, on which boats could be used to carry the corn, wheat, flax, and wool down to the market towns on the coast. There these products would be traded for the salt, iron, tea, tools, and other things that farmers needed.

Great-grandfather McCormick had lived on a farm in Pennsylvania. On this farm he plowed and harvested the grain with the farm tools he had brought with him from his home in Europe. In those early days there were no machines such as we have today to help with the farm work; in fact, farmers were just beginning to discover new ways of making hand tools that could do more work than the old tools their forefathers had used.

The design of these farm tools was very, very old. The plow with which Great-grandfather McCormick broke his ground and the sickles with which he cut his grain were like the plows and sickles the farmers of Egypt over a thousand years before had used on their farms along the banks of the Nile River. The short scythes used on the McCormick place were almost exactly like the scythes used on the old farms of Rome.

When Great-grandfather McCormick's son grew up and wanted a farm of his own, there was little good land left on any of the rivers or streams near his father's home. So the McCormick son took his tools and went off across the Indian trails, through the forest and over the hills, and came out on the banks of the Shenandoah River in Virginia. Here there was still plenty of land to be had for nothing. He cut down trees and built himself a log house; then he plowed his newly cleared land and planted it with corn and wheat. The land was rich, and it grew splendid crops. Everything went well with the young McCormick family. As time went on, the family grew bigger and bigger, and the McCormick farm spread out over more and more land.

This great Virginia farm had broad fields of oats, corn, wheat, and other grains; beautiful pastures with strong, fine horses, good cows, and fleecy sheep; and large barnyards of hens, ducks, and geese. There were two gristmills for grinding the McCormicks' and their neighbors' grain into flour and meal. Two sawmills quickly turned logs into broad planks and stout boards. A smelting furnace turned iron ore from the nearby mountain into lumps of pure iron all ready for the farm's blacksmith to hammer into horseshoes, pincers, tongs, crowbars, hammers, and other tools needed on the farm. They spun and wove their own cloth and made it into clothing; they made their own soap and candles, dyes, hogsheads, barrels, tubs, and vats. In fact, that old McCormick family, like all other farmers of the time, did nearly everything for themselves.

Every year they plowed and planted; and every year when the grain was ripe, every man, woman, and child of the McCormick family went out into the fields to help bring in the crop.

How everyone did work! The harvest season was so short that there was not a single minute to waste if the precious grain was to be put under cover before the fall storms came. Rain, wind, and sunshine are good for grain all through the long months of the growing season, but rain, wind, and too much sunshine are anything but good for grain that is tall and ripe. And so the moment the grain was ripe enough to be cut, the whole family went into the fields and worked from daylight until dark. They hastened to get their harvest in before the storms overtook them, or before the warm sun over-ripened the seeds so that they fell to the ground.

The men with sickles went ahead. They held a bunch of grain with one hand, swung the sickle with the other, and let the stalks fall to the ground as they cut their way across the field. Each man with a sickle was followed by another worker who gathered up the fallen stalks, tied them into bundles, and tossed them back to the ground. The men who had the scythes with long handles and blades did not need to hold the grain as they cut it. They used both hands to swing the scythes, and they cut a wider path through the grain as they worked their way across the fields.

The tools that the McCormick son and his neighbors used in harvesting their crops were the same as those used by Great-grandfather McCormick on his farm back in Pennsylvania. After using such tools for many years, the son bought a scythe that he had seen the farmers along the coast using to harvest their grain. They called the new kind of scythe a cradle scythe because it had long wooden fingers on the handle just above the knife. These fingers cradled, or held, the grain until the knife had finished its work; then they laid it in neat rows to one side.

Fifty years went by, and the sons and grandsons of the first McCormick who had settled in the Shenandoah Valley were still harvesting their grain with the cradle scythe. One of the McCormick sons spent every spare moment of his time in his workshop. There he had discovered several ways of making many of the old farm tools into new tools that did a great deal more work than any of the old ones had ever done.

As this man went about the country, however, and saw field after field of ripe grain that could not possibly be cut and gathered in time to save it, he began to see that men with hand tools alone could not keep up with the huge crops the rich farmlands were producing. Some kind of harvesting machine was needed. So he began to study and plan and work. When his machine was finally finished, he and his son Cyrus Hall McCormick tried it out in one of their fields. But something was wrong; the machine trampled down the grain instead of cutting it.

Then Cyrus Hall McCormick began experimenting with his father's machine. After many trials, he sent out word one day to the farmers that he had made a reaping machine. He invited them to come and see it work. More than a hundred neighbors gathered at Farmer Ruff's field, where the machine was to be tried out. The reaping machine, pulled by a single draft horse, rattled and clattered as Cyrus Hall McCormick drove it out of the barn and into the field. Dogs barked and boys yelled and whistled as the machine rattled clumsily along. The farm hands chuckled and laughed; farmers grinned and shook their heads in disbelief. They did not believe that such an awkward-looking machine could ever cut grain, and they did not hesitate to say what they thought.

The field was rough and hilly. Jolting and jerking from side to side, the reaping machine cut the grain in such irregular fashion that Farmer Ruff ordered Cyrus Hall McCormick to stop what he was doing and cease ruining his field of wheat. A bystander shouted to McCormick, "Pull down that fence; drive over into my field and try your machine there." In that field, which was smooth and level, Cyrus Hall McCormick's machine cut six acres of oats easily before the sun went down! The crowd of onlookers was astounded!

The new machine could do all the work of cutting grain. It had a divider that separated the grain to be cut from the grain left standing. It had fingers that caught

and held the stalks while the knife blade moved back and forth, cutting with each stroke. In fact, it had almost all the main parts of the reaping machines we use on our farms today. The McCormick farm of the Shenandoah Valley had made history, and the first major step toward mechanized farming was taken. Because of modern farm machinery, there is food today for millions of people who would otherwise go hungry.

51

It Is Common

The anonymous American poet who wrote these lines expresses the thought that the best things of life are really the commonest, if we could only be persuaded of this.

So are the stars and the arching skies,
So are the smiles in the children's eyes;
Common the life-giving breath of the spring;
So are the songs which the wild birds sing—
　　Blessed be God, they are common!

Common the grass in its glowing green;
So is the water's glistening sheen;
Common the springs of love and mirth;
So are the holiest gifts of earth.

Common the fragrance of rosy June;
So is the generous harvest moon,
So are the towering, mighty hills,
So the meandering, trickling rills.

Common the beautiful tints of the fall;
So is the sun which is over all.
Common the rain with its pattering feet;
So is the bread which we daily eat—
　　Blessed be God, it is common!

So is the sea in its wild unrest,
Common the grace wherewith we are blessed;
So unto all are the promises given,
So unto all is the hope of heaven—
  Blessed be God, it is common!

AUTHOR UNKNOWN

52

 The Fox Den

BY WILLIAM J. LONG

One day last spring I found a new fox den in the woods. Since then it has been good fun to see the cubs playing games that look like versions of hide-and-seek, tag, "king of the castle," and several others that have no names, all in a pleasant morning or afternoon.

How did I find it, you ask? Most fox dens are so well concealed that you must search a long while, and perhaps get a hound dog to help, before you find one; but this time I was not looking for dens or thinking of foxes. It happened that I was sitting on a log by a little brook, watching a pair of birds built their nest, when a mother fox came trotting along as if she did not see me.

The old mother fox saw me plainly enough; this I could tell by the crafty look in her eyes. Instead of running off, though, she began to act in a way that made me think of the pretty trick which a mother quail or a mother partridge plays to outwit you when you come near her chicks.

You know how these brave little mother birds act at such a time—how they deliberately throw themselves at your feet, clucking or squealing as if they were hurt, and how they flap along the ground as if they could not run or fly. They want you to follow (as I hope you always will), and when you do follow, they lead you away from where the chicks are hiding. Then *whir-r-r!*—away they go and are out of sight in a twinkling.

So it happened, when the mother fox sat down only a few yards away and turned her back and scratched an ear with a hind foot, that I began for the first time to understand her. "She has been watching me," was my thought. "She must have a den near here and she wants to lure me away from it. Now let's keep still and see what she will do."

When I paid no attention to her ear scratching—or when she thought so—the mother fox turned to face me and opened her mouth in a wide yawn, as your dog does when he wants you to do something, or as some people do when they are sleepy and forget their manners. Again she opened her mouth wide, showing all her sharp teeth and her slender red tongue, and this time I heard the low whine that goes with a yawn—*eeee-ou-ow!* When that failed to make me move, she began to bark or yap at me, like a small dog that is trying to express what he thinks of you.

At this, I had to show her some attention; she was so insisting in her own way. "Here I am; catch me if you can," she seemed to be saying. Her ears were up and her eyes very bright when I rose to my feet, as if surprised; and to please her I followed as she trotted away, catching a glimpse of yellow fur now and then till we came to a great rocky ledge that rose above the treetops like a mountain. When the mother fox was lost among the rocks, I went back and found her den, only a little way from where the birds were building their nest.

After that it was very pleasant to discreetly observe

the little troupe and learn that the daytime of a young fox (I can't tell you much about his nights) is divided into three parts: eating, sleeping, and playing. Eating takes but a few minutes; sleeping calls for three or four hours; and the rest of every fine day, which means the largest part, is given to play. And you do not have to watch fox cubs very long to know that they are happy little players.

A good time to watch the den is in the early morning before sunrise. For then you may sometimes see the mother fox come with a catch of field mice hanging from her pointed jaws. She makes no call or outcry, but somehow the cubs know she is coming and out they tumble to meet her. The mother distributes the mice; each hungry little fellow gets his share, and in a moment it is gone. Never a scrap is left to tell what they have devoured. Fox cubs seem to like mice better than any other food, and they never have enough; or so you may think, seeing them gobble a dozen and then go sniffing about as if hoping to find a few more.

Soon after breakfast the cubs go into the den, but the mother fox does not join them there except in a storm (when they all sleep the whole day long). In pleasant weather she curls up on a rock or a stump near the entrance of the den to rest till sunset. She looks hungry, and no doubt she is: the best of her hunting always goes to her cubs.

This latest den of mine, you should know, is in a secluded bank within sight of an old woods road that is no longer used by men. Near the mouth of the den is the stump of a tree, and close around the roots of the stump is a circular path, a path trampled in the earth by the running of little feet. Touching this path on the north side of the stump is a larger ring, about four feet across, worn in the dead leaves by the same little feet; and touching the path on the south or opposite side is another ring. Around these rings the cubs play a nameless game of some kind, a game that is hard for us to follow because we have nothing like it.

While the merry little fellows play silently, hour after hour, the old mother fox, or vixen as hunters call her, is stretched out on a flat rock above them, keeping watch. Her eyes look sleepy but her sensitive ears and nose are wide awake. Suddenly a dog barks, and the vixen's eyes snap abruptly open! A second bark is heard, this time nearer. Now the vixen lifts her head and points her ears at the cubs. She makes no outcry, no sound of any kind that your ears can hear, but at this gesture the cubs quit their play and slip like shadows into the den.

As the last little tail goes underground, the vixen leaps far out from her rock and makes a swift circle of tracks entirely around the den and playground. Any dog, smelling these fresh tracks first, will naturally follow them and so learn nothing of the cubs. If he comes too near, the vixen will show herself in plain sight and *yap-yap* at him until he chases her. So she lures him off to the great ledge, where she squeezes into a tiny den under the rocks. If the dog is small and foolish enough to follow her, he gets his nose nipped by sharp teeth for his folly, and a big dog gets only sore feet from trying to scratch away a mountain with his toenails.

Once you have seen the play ended for any reason, go away quietly and be content with what you have seen. You may come back another day and renew your watching, so long as you keep at a distance. But you should never examine the den closely or leave the scent of your feet on the playground more than once; otherwise, the vixen will know that you have found her den. Then she may take her cubs far away to a safer place, carrying them one by one in her mouth as a cat a carries her kittens.

53

 The Answer for Niklaus

BY JOYCE ZIMMERMAN

"Hi! Ho! Up the hill to the pasture!" fifteen-year-old Niklaus called as he darted here and there, waving his cowherd's stick. Skillfully he herded his family's ten Brown Swiss milk cows out of the stable.

It was early morning, and with milking finished, it was his chore to drive the herd up the mountain trail to their springtime pasture on the alp. No time could be lost; the cattle had to be over the steep slopes to the pasture before the day became warm. Niklaus's rosy-cheeked sister, Maria, came running toward him with a knapsack containing his lunch.

"God be with you, Niklaus," his mother called with a wave and a smile from the doorway of the house.

"And with you, Mother," he called back cheerily. To Maria he said, "Perhaps you can come with me to the high pasture some day when Mother doesn't need you to help her."

The golden-haired child smiled happily, nodded her head vigorously, and ran back to the house.

Niklaus was eager to be on his way. He had some

serious thinking to do today, and nowhere could he think more clearly than in the pure, fresh air of the high pasture. As the cows turned onto the trail and began the ascent, Niklaus fell in behind them, swinging his stick and whistling a tune.

Ever since he had been old enough to be trusted with the responsibility, Niklaus Andersen had been a cowherd. His family spent the winters on a lower slope near the tiny village where Niklaus and Maria attended school. It was not until the rain and warm winds of spring had melted the snow from the high pastures, that the family loaded their belongings onto carts and moved to their chalet on the hillside. From there the cattle had a shorter climb to the alpine pastures. The days in the high country were spent tending the cows and making cheese, as well as cutting and storing hay made from the sweet grass on the slopes. This hay was used to feed the cattle during the long winter season spent in the lowlands.

After a time, Niklaus let the cows go on alone while he clambered onto his favorite perch, a large rock by the trail. From here he could look down and see the entire valley below him, neatly divided into winter pastures and summer gardens and dotted with the brightly colored roofs of farm buildings and cottages. The first rays of the morning sun were just touching the lowlands, and here and there a dashing stream reflected their glow as it hurried toward the river in the valley bottom. Snowcaps and glaciers topped the jagged peaks that rose from the valley floor. A short distance below him, in the cool shadow of the morning, was Niklaus's own home. The faint tinkling and clanging of pots and pans told him that his parents were already busy, making cheese from the morning's milk.

His gaze returning to the lowlands, Niklaus could

see the peaked roof of the house where his friend Franz lived. "Yes," Niklaus thought, "I have some serious thinking to do today." Like him, Franz was also a cowherd. The two boys had spent many happy hours together on the alps, but this year Niklaus would be alone with his family's cattle. Only last night, he had learned that Franz's father had sold his herd and was planning to move his family into one of the large towns where industry was booming. He claimed that it was too hard and too dangerous to make a living in the old way.

"Times have changed," he had told Mr. Andersen, "and there is easier money to be made in the factories. Why should we wear ourselves out here in these treacherous mountains?"

When Niklaus's father had told him that Franz would not be returning to the mountain that year, Niklaus was stunned. Leaving the alps! It was hard to imagine such a thing. What would life be like without the gentle cows, the rich pastures carpeted with wildflowers, and the exhilarating air of the heights?

Niklaus dropped from the rock and hastened along to join the cattle, troubled by the thought of his friend's departure.

At length he climbed the last rocky steps of the trail up the mountain. Before him a wide meadow opened out, with snow-topped peaks rising on all sides. The cattle were soon grazing. Niklaus found a comfortable spot from where he could watch them, and there he sat down to continue his thinking.

He recalled the words of Franz's father's. "Why should we wear ourselves out here in these treacherous mountains?"

"Is our life in the mountains really so hard and dangerous?" the boy wondered. He thought of the possibility of wandering too close to the edge of a cliff and falling into a rocky chasm or a rushing torrent far below, and of how easily one could become lost in the mountains during a snowstorm or when heavy fogs descended. Glancing upward toward the highest of the peaks, he saw clouds of snow rising and falling along the mountain ridges. A severe storm was raging there in spite of the pleasant day. He thought of the glacier edges where immense columns of ice were suspended, split away from the larger masses and ready to topple onto unwary travelers. He shivered as he recalled the many times he had heard the crashing and roaring of slides in the mountains. Yes, Franz's father was right; the high places could be dangerous.

A sudden movement caught Niklaus's eye. A marmot had appeared as if from nowhere. Seeing Niklaus, it turned and scurried quickly away to lose itself among the rocks. Niklaus laughed, glad to be drawn from his unpleasant musings. He looked again toward the tall peaks rising above him; the clouds had disappeared from their summits. Now they seemed to smile down at him in a friendly, protective way. He thought of the opening of the psalm that his father had read aloud the evening before.

"I will lift up mine eyes unto the hills, from whence cometh my help."

A feeling of reassurance came over him as he repeated the line aloud. Niklaus sensed that life in the city could never be as peaceful as his life in the mountains.

He would miss Franz, of that he was sure. In fact, he missed him already. As he reached for his knapsack containing his lunch of bread and cheese, he suddenly felt very sorry for his friend. To leave the mountains and move to the city simply because it would be easier to earn a living . . . Niklaus could not understand this.

Niklaus finished his simple lunch and then took a

walk, circling the grazing cattle to assure himself that all was well. Returning to his lunch place, he took a carving knife and a partly finished wooden bowl from his knapsack and began to whittle. Occasionally he reached out and picked one of the delicate spring flowers that nodded their lovely heads near him. He would take a bouquet home to Maria.

Before long, the shadows began to lengthen. Niklaus raised his wooden horn to his lips and sounded several long notes to call the cows together. He could hear other cowherds calling on other slopes. The notes mingled and reverberated among the mountains to mark the end of the day for the herd boys.

Niklaus collected his cattle and started down the slope to the stable, where his father would be ready for the evening milking. No, Niklaus thought, a desire for an easy living or fear of his beloved mountains would not draw him away. His joyous whistling blended with the jingling of the cowbells as he descended the homeward way.

54

With Wings as Eagles

Hast thou not known? hast thou not heard,
That the everlasting God, the LORD,
The Creator of the ends of the earth,
Fainteth not, neither is weary?
There is no searching of his understanding.

He giveth power to the faint;
And to them that have no might he increaseth
strength.
Even the youths shall faint and be weary,
And the young men shall utterly fall:

But they that wait upon the LORD
Shall renew their strength;
They shall mount up with wings as eagles;
They shall run, and not be weary;
And they shall walk, and not faint.

ISAIAH 40:28–31

55

 Brother David's Song

BY MAUREEN HUBER

Quietly Jill stepped a little closer to her mother's side. "Maybe I can get her attention without having to interrupt the conversation," she thought, waiting patiently.

Before long, Mother glanced her way, her eyebrows raised in question. Jill beckoned, and Mother moved a little away from the group of sisters with whom she had been talking. The service had ended some time ago, but no one had made any move to leave the building. All enjoyed the time of fellowship after the meeting.

"Mother," Jill kept her voice low, "Sister Rhoda is trying to find some girls who can go with her for lunch and then go singing for some older folks whom she knows. She asked me to go along."

Mother thought a moment. "I don't know why not," she replied. "Does she need an answer right away? We ld check with Father."

ll nodded. "If you would rather I didn't go, she ike to know so she can ask someone else."

ight," Mother consented. "I'll check with Father ." And she started toward the men's side of the

"Bless her," Jill thought to herself. "She knows I'm too bashful to go over where all the men are to ask for myself. Especially with our being new here."

Soon Mother returned. "Yes, you may go," she gave the hoped-for answer. "Be a good girl," she concluded with a smile.

Jill smiled back and nodded. Then she was off to find Sister Rhoda.

After an enjoyable dinner, Sister Rhoda and the five girls who accompanied her arrived at the home of an elderly bishop who lived with his married son's family. "I guess some of you have never met Brother David," Sister Rhoda said as she looked over her group of singers. "I shall warn you that he is very forgetful, for his mind doesn't work properly. Don't be surprised if he asks for the same song a number of times." And so saying, she turned and led the way to the front door.

"Come in! Come in!" the trembling voice greeted as Brother David's son led the way to the living room, where the old man lay resting on a sofa.

"He sounds so glad to see us," Jill thought to herself. "I wonder if he doesn't get much company?" she whispered to the girl by her side before they reached the living room.

Alma shook her head. "Apparently not. It seems that since he's senile, he has very few visitors. And he's so glad when someone does come that I really wonder why more folks don't visit him."

Jill nodded. "He can't help it that he doesn't have a strong mind anymore," she agreed softly.

Speaking clearly so the time-dulled ears would not miss what she said, Sister Rhoda introduced each of the girls to Brother David. He had met most of them before, but he could never remember their names and often forgot their faces too. He always remembered

Sister Rhoda, though, because he had known her for many years before his mind had become undependable.

As Jill shook hands with him, he said uncertainly, "I've never seen you before, have I?"

She smiled sweetly. "No, we just moved here," she explained. "But I'm glad Sister Rhoda asked me to come. Since we moved, my own grandfather is not nearby as he was before. So I will enjoy visiting with you instead."

"Thank you," he said simply, and Jill noticed that there were tears in his eyes. "Sit here close to me," he invited.

Smiling, Jill sat on the chair nearest him. "My own grandchildren are so busy, they don't very often have any time for me," he explained. "I'm glad you folks came."

"We thought maybe you'd like to have us sing with you awhile," Sister Rhoda offered.

Brother David's face lit up again. "Oh, yes. I miss the singing so much since I can't get to church anymore."

Sister Rhoda distributed the hymnbooks that she had left on a table near the door. "Let's start with 'The Lord My Shepherd Is,'" she suggested.

The girls sang happily, and Brother David's tremulous voice joined them occasionally. Soon that song was finished. "Now, Brother, perhaps you have a favorite that you would like to sing?" Sister Rhoda asked.

"Oh, yes," he answered quickly. "Do you know the one, 'When the Roll Is Called Up Yonder'?" They all nodded and began the first stanza. Brother David's eyes filled again as they sang. Jill could tell that he was waiting for the day when the roll would be called, and she liked the tone of his voice when he sang the last phrase, "I'll be there."

When the song was finished, Sister Rhoda asked if any of the girls had a selection they would like to sing. Someone suggested "Safe in the Arms of Jesus." They could all tell that Brother David was moved by the words as they sang:

Here let me wait with patience,
Wait till the night is o'er;
Wait till I see the morning
Break on the golden shore.

"True, his memory is poor, but he hasn't forgotten the hope of his former years," Jill pondered. "Obviously, he's just waiting for that day to break for him."

"Now, Brother David, perhaps you have another selection," Sister Rhoda suggested again.

The elderly man looked thoughtful. "What you just sang makes me think of the song, 'When the Roll Is Called Up Yonder.' Do you girls know it?" he asked hopefully.

They all nodded. Jill was glad to see that the other girls did not let on that they had just sung it. Once again their voices rose in the familiar strains, and Brother David joined them in the chorus. " 'When the roll is called up yonder, *I'll be there.*' "

Once more the three stanzas were completed. "Now," Sister Rhoda suggested, " I think we'll sing 'The Old Rugged Cross.' Brother David, you like that one, don't you?"

"Yes," he nodded happily. "Please do sing it."

They sang heartily, and once again the trembling voice joined in the chorus.

"Now, Brother, do you have another selection that you would enjoy?" Sister Rhoda inquired when they had finished.

He looked thoughtful awhile. "Well, yes," he said slowly. "Would you girls know, 'When the Roll Is Called Up Yonder'?"

Sister Rhoda smiled understandingly as she answered, "Yes, I think we all know it. Does someone have the number?"

They sang for about an hour and a half, during which time they sang "When the Roll Is Called Up Yonder" five times. After visiting a little longer, Sister Rhoda suggested, "Now I think it is time for us to move along. We have another place to go yet this afternoon." Soon they had all said good-bye and were on their way.

"Well, Jill," Sister Rhoda inquired of the girl at her side as they drove out the lane, "how did you like singing for Brother David?"

"I enjoyed it," the girl answered. "Of course, it seemed strange to sing the same song over and over, but I'm sure he did not realize that we'd already sung it. And he enjoyed it so much every time."

"That's what he always does," one of the other girls explained. "We've gotten used to it, and we don't mind either. I guess we really should go and visit him more often," she added. "I think it's good for him, and it's a real lesson in patience for us."

"You're right, Louise," Sister Rhoda agreed. "He's been more and more neglected the past few years. I think one of the reasons folks don't go to visit him more is that they are embarrassed by his forgetfulness. I've heard a number of people say, 'If only he wasn't so forgetful.' I agree with Louise. If we were as patient as we ought to be, it wouldn't bother us."

"And if we're not as patient as we ought to be, perhaps more frequent visits with Brother David would increase our patience," Jill suggested, silently resolving to ask her whole family to visit Brother David soon. She knew he would really enjoy it.

"That's right, Jill," Sister Rhoda encouraged. "The Bible tells us to 'be patient toward all men,' and it doesn't make any exception."

"Not even if they want us to sing 'When the Roll Is Called Up Yonder' five times in a little over an hour," Jill concluded pleasantly. "I'm glad we went. Let's do it again soon."

56

 Language Without *Love*

BY VIOLET WOOD

"Onka na?" The American missionary pointed with his long, slender finger at the kerosene lamp. "What is that?" he had asked in Mongo-Nkundo. Andrew F. Hensey, with pencil and notebook in hand, was beginning the task of writing down words that had never before been reduced to writing—laborious words spoken daily by the Bantu people of Bolenge and neighboring districts on the Congo River in central Africa. The year was 1906.

The big black man, bangled and barefooted, with strips of leopard skin on his hair and around his waist, answered the missionary, *"Bosai."*

There was a bench on the porch where Hensey was working. He pointed his finger at it and repeated the question. "Onka na?"

"Bosai," said the chief, his eyes flashing in a broad smile.

Bosai—lamp! Bosai—bench! Funny, thought Hensey, that right off he should have picked identical-sounding words.

He turned to one of the chief's wives. Pointing at the banana tree in the mission yard, he repeated, "Onka na?"

"Bosai!" The woman was grinning too!

Desperately, Hensey got up and went over to a small boy. Pointing his finger at the woman, he asked loudly, "Onka na?"

"Bosai! Bosai! Bosai!" the boy shouted. He was shaking with laughter, and so were all the others.

Oh, it was a delicious joke! Ruefully Hensey had to laugh too. The only trouble was, Hensey did not know what he was laughing at. It was a serious matter for him as well as for the whole missionary enterprise. If the answer to "What is that?" could only be "Bosai," and this word was some kind of joke among these primitive people, how could the missionaries break through to the language?

The Mongo-Nkundo language had no written alphabet and therefore no grammar, no dictionary, no book of any kind that Hensey could consult in his search for words. He had set about with his colleagues to record the language from the speech of the people. But *bosai* had them stopped cold. How could they ever learn a language where the name of everything was bosai?

It was weeks before Hensey found out by accident that *bosai* was the word for finger. Every time he pointed, the Africans thought that he wanted to know the name for *finger* and that he was playing some kind of white man's game. When you point at something in the Congo, you stick your lower lip out at it.

And so Hensey and his missionary colleagues went around shooting out their lower lip at trees, animals, birds, and so on, accumulating words for the wonders of this fascinating land of canoe gypsies and hippopotamus hunters. That was fine for nouns, but how could anybody stick out his lower lip at a verb, an adverb, or an idea—like *sit, quickly,* or *love?*

Hensey wore himself out, performing verb pantomimes. With their mouths wide open, the Africans watched him sit, stand, run, sit, stand, run in rapid succession until they got the idea and cried, "kitsanse," "emala," "ukumwa." To get adverbs, Hensey did it all over again with modifications: sitting slowly, running fast, and so forth. But there was still the problem of finding words for ideas, and words to express the Christian vocabulary that was beyond the experience of the Africans. This was a riddle that could be solved only by years of living with the people. The word *love,* used more times in the Bible than in any other religious book, and the words *hope* and *peace*—none of these seemed to exist in Mongo-Nkundo. No one ever said "I love" or "I hope."

Hensey spent years patiently recording the words that he learned. He tracked them down in jungle greenery, at dances in the village clearings, by the bedsides of those stricken with tropical sicknesses, and in the canoe whose calling card at every shore was relayed by drumbeat. But he still had no word for *love.* There was an expression that he heard the Bantu mothers use in speaking tenderly to their own littlest children: "ok'eefe." He asked one day, "Ooi na *ok'eefe?*"

"Bondele [white man]," the mother said, *"ok'eefe* means that I care for this little girl of mine so much that when I think of what is going to befall her when she grows up . . . it hurts me."

"Caring so much that it hurts"—Hensey had at last discovered the Bantu concept for love.

Since there was no writing among the people, the word for *write,* of course, was nonexistent. It was adopted from the chance speech of a small boy who watched Hensey writing with a stick in the dust of the street the bold outline of the first letter of the alphabet.

The street was the scene of many an early mission lesson in reading and writing before slates arrived from America and before schools were built.

"Come quickly!" cried the little boy to his loitering brothers. "Our Bondele is cutting tribal marks in the sand."

The boy had said the word *kota*, used by the "artists in blood" who cut into the living flesh of the faces and bodies of little children the intricate designs by which all men might know their tribe. Today in Christian Bolenge and the surrounding districts, as a result of the work of Hensey and his colleagues, birth certificates take the place of the barbaric practice of tribal branding.

There were other problems to be overcome—deep-rooted fears and superstitions that obstructed knowledge.

One day a fierce warrior called on Hensey, who happened to be writing a letter to his mission board. "What are you doing, *Nkökö?*" the chief asked. *Nkökö*, which means "grandfather," was Hensey's African name even though he was then a very young man.

"I am telling my people at home in Indianapolis, many, many rivers away, about the beauty of your country and the need of your people for the good tidings of Jesus. Two moons will wane before these words come to my land."

The chief banged his tribal stick on the floor. His black eyes rolled and his nostrils widened in anger. "You are lying, Bondele. You cannot make paper run away and talk!"

"I will prove it to you," said Hensey quietly. "I will write on this paper anything you tell me. You may take it to the Bondele in the other house, and he will tell you what it says."

"Write," commanded the old chief craftily, " 'Give this chief six oranges.' "

Hensey wrote down the request and put it in the split end of the chief's stick. The chief was afraid to touch the paper with his hands. Waving it like a flag, the chief went next door to the house of the other missionary. The white man took the note, read it quickly, and called out to one of the family, "Give this chief six oranges!"

The chief never got his oranges. He fled down the path to spread among his people the terror of "the paper that really could talk!"

After Hensey and the other missionaries had acquired the language, and long before any of the people had been taught to read it, the missionaries preached and told the stories of he Bible. Seated at evening under the tropic moon, around the fire in the village clearing, the missionaries passed on to the Bantus—as their chiefs and storytellers had for centuries passed on the traditional knowledge of the tribe—the message they had come so far to share.

When the time for Bible translation finally came, the missionaries still had a thousand problems to face. "Wash me, and I shall be whiter than snow" and "his raiment white as snow" were two of them. How should David's prayer for cleansing, and the description of the angel who rolled away the stone from Jesus' tomb, be translated into Mongo-Nkundo? These Africans had never seen snow. Nor ice! Nor frost! But egrets, great-winged birds caught in gleaming flight under the tropic sun—they were the whitest white the Africans knew. "Wash me, and I shall be whiter than egrets" and "his raiment white as egrets" are two phrases in the Mongo-Nkundo Bible that differ from ours.

Consider the wolves of Arabia that wander through the Old and New Testaments, preying upon lambs—how should that be translated in a land where there are no wolves? But the leopard is common, a constant danger to sheep and little children. And the passage from Luke reads in Mongo-Nkundo, "I send you forth as lambs among leopards."

Candlestick, tents, desert, window, steps, and *three-story houses,* in a land that knows none of these things, become "holder-of-torches," "cloth houses," "dry country," "small door," "short up-paths," and "three-houses-high." Just as we have many beautiful idioms in English, Hensey discovered some picturesque speech among the Bantus. One expression is particularly eloquent. When you kick a man in Congoland, you "stab him with a footprint."

All these problems were finally solved, the Bible was translated, printed, and ready to deliver—but what good was accomplished if the people could not read? Side by side with the tremendous task of translation, Hensey had carried on the equally tremendous task of education. By the time the New Testament was ready in 1921, the children of the chief who had been afraid to touch "talking paper" could read and write, and about a thousand others of his tribe had also learned.

The day that Andrew Hensey left Africa, eight hundred Christian Africans gathered on the shore of the Congo River to wish Godspeed to their departing teacher and friend. *"Yawi Fafa, otobatele enjiman iso endoko* [God be with you till we meet again]," they sang.

57

Sleep Sweet

Sleep sweet within this quiet room,
　　O thou, whoe'er thou art,
And let no mournful yesterdays
　　Disturb thy peaceful heart.

Nor let tomorrow mar thy rest
　　With dreams of coming ill:
Thy Maker is thy changeless friend,
　　His love surrounds thee still.

Forget thyself and all the world,
　　Put out each garish light:
The stars are shining overhead—
　　Sleep sweet! Good night! Good night!

ELLEN M. HUNTINGTON GATES

58

 ## The Mother Teal
and the Overland Route

BY ERNEST THOMPSON SETON

Part I

A green-winged teal had made her nest in the sedge by one of the grass-edged pools that fleck the sunny slope of Riding Mountain. The passing farm hand, driving his creaking ox wagon, saw only a pond with the usual fringe of coarse grass, beyond which were a belt of willow scrub and an old poplar tree. But the little teal in the rushes and her neighbors, the flickers on the nearby poplar, saw in the nestling pool a kingdom, a perfect paradise, for this was home. And spring was at its fullest.

Indeed, the little flickers had almost chipped their glassy shells, and the eggs, the ten treasures of the teal, had lost the look of mere interesting things. They were each putting on an air of sleeping personality, warm, pulsatory, almost vocal.

The little teal had lost her mate early in the season. At least, he had disappeared, and as the land abounded in deadly foes, it was fair to suppose him dead. But her attention was fully taken up with her nest and her brood.

All through the latter part of June, she tended them

238

carefully. She left but a little while each day to seek food after covering them carefully with a dummy foster mother that she had made of down from her own breast.

One morning as she flew away, leaving the dummy in charge, she heard an ominous crackling in the thick willows near at hand, but she wisely went on. When she returned, her neighbor, the flicker, was still uttering a note of alarm, and down by her own nest were fresh tracks of a man. The dummy mother had been disturbed, but strange to tell, the eggs were all there and unharmed.

The enemy, though so near, had been baffled after all. As the days went by and the grand finish of her task drew near, the little green-wing felt the mother love growing in her heart, to be ready for the ten little prisoners that her devotion was to set free. They were no longer mere eggs, she felt, and sometimes she would talk to them in low, crooning tones. They would seem to answer from within in whispered peepings, or perhaps in sounds that have no human name because they are too fine for human ears. So there is small wonder that when they do come out, they have already learned many of the simple words that make up teal talk.

The many hazards of the early nesting time were rapidly passed, but a new one came. The growing springtime had turned into a drought. No rain had fallen for many, many days, and as the greatest day of all drew near, the mother saw with dismay that the pond was shrinking, quickly shrinking. Already it was rimmed about by a great stretch of bare mud, and unless the rains came soon, the first experience of the little ones would be a perilous overland journey.

It was just as impossible to hurry up the hatching as it was to bring rain, and the last few days of the mother's task were, as she had feared, in view of a wide mud flat where once had been the pond.

They all came out at last. The little china tombs were broken one by one, each disclosing a little teal: ten little balls of mottled down, ten little cushions of yellow plush, ten little golden caskets with jewel eyes, each enshrining a priceless spark of life.

It was now a matter of life and death to reach a pond. Oh, why could not the downlings have three days of paddling to strengthen on before enforcing this dreadful

journey overland? But the mother must face the problem and face it now, or lose them all.

Ducklings do not need to eat for several hours after they hatch. Their bodies are yet sustained by the nourishment of their last abode. But once that is used, they must eat. The nearest pond was half a mile away. And the great questions were: Can these baby ducks hold out that long? Can they escape the countless dangers of the road? For not a harrier, falcon, hawk, fox, weasel, coyote, gopher, ground squirrel, or snake but would count them his lawful prey.

All this the mother felt instinctively, even if she could not set it forth in clear expression; and as soon as the ten were warmed and lively, she led them into the grass. Such a scrambling and peeping and tumbling about as they tried to get through and over the grass stalks that barred their way like a bamboo forest! Their mother had to watch the ten with one eye and the whole world with the other, for not a friend had she or they outside of themselves. The countless living things about were either foes or neutral.

PART II

After a long scramble through the grass, they climbed a bank and got among the willow scrub and here sat down to rest. One little fellow that had struggled along bravely with the others was so weak that there seemed no chance of his reaching that faraway haven, the pond.

When they were rested, their mother gave a low, gentle *quack* that doubtless meant, "Come along, children." So they set off again, scrambling over and around the twigs, each peeping softly when he was getting along nicely, or plaintively when he found himself caught in some thicket.

At last they came to a wide open place. It was easy to travel here, but there was great danger of hawks. The mother rested long in the edge of the thicket, and scanned the sky in every direction before she ventured into the open. Then, when all was clear, she marshaled her little ones for a dash over this great desert of nearly one hundred yards.

The little fellows struggled bravely after her, their

small yellow bodies raised at an angle and their tiny wings held out like arms as they pushed along after their mother.

She was anxious to finish it all at one dash, but she soon saw that that was hopeless. The strongest of her brood could keep up with her, but the others dragged in order of weakness. Nine of them now formed a little procession over twenty feet long, with the weakling another ten feet behind that.

A dangerous rest in the open would be necessary. The peepers came panting up to their mother; and full of anxiety, she lay there beside them until they were able to go on. Then she led them as before, quacking gently, "Courage, my darlings!"

They were not halfway to the pond yet, and the journey was already telling on them. The brood was strung out into another long procession, with a wide gap to the runt in the rear, when a great marsh hawk suddenly appeared, skimming low over the ground.

"Squat!" gasped Mother Green-wing, and the little things all lay flat except the last one. Too far off to hear the warning, he struggled on. The great hawk swooped, seized him in his claws, and carried him peeping away over the bushes. All the poor mother could do was gaze in dumb sorrow as the bloodthirsty pirate bore off the downling, unresisted and unpunished. Yet not entirely; for as he flew straight to the bank of the pond where dwelt his crew of young marauders, he heedlessly passed over the home bush of a kingbird, and that fearless little warrior screamed out his battle cry as he launched into the air to give chase. Away went the pirate and away went the king, the one huge, heavy, and cowardly, the other small, swift, and fearless as a hero—away and away, out of sight, the kingbird gaining at every stroke until his voice was lost in the distance.

The sorrow of Mother Green-wing, if less deep than that of the human mother, was yet very real. But she still had the nine to guard. They needed her every thought. She led them as quickly as possible into the bushes, and for a time they breathed more freely.

Thenceforth she managed to have the journey lie through cover. An hour or more passed by in slight alarms and in many rests, but at last the pond was near. And well it was, for the ducklings were almost worn out, their little paddles scratched and bleeding, their strength all but gone. For a time they gasped under the shadow of the last tall bush before again setting out in a compact flock to cross the next bare place, a rough opening through the willows.

They never knew that death in another form had hovered on their track. A red fox crossed the trail of the little duck family. His keen nose told him at once that here was a feast awaiting, and all he had to do was follow it up and eat. So he sneaked softly and swiftly along their well-marked trail until he came in sight of them. In the ordinary course he soon would have had them, mother and all, but the ordinary course may go askew. He was near enough to count the little travelers, if count he could, when the wind brought something that made him stop and crouch low. Then at a surer whiff he slunk away, fleeing as swiftly as he could without being seen. So the greatest danger, surest death of all that had threatened, was thwarted by an unseen power, and not even the watchful mother duck had the slightest hint of it.

PART III

The little ones now toddled along after their mother, who led them quickly to cross the opening. To her delight, a long arm of the pond was quite close, just

244

across that treeless lane. She made straight for it, joy-
fully calling, "Come, my darlings!"

But alas! The treeless opening was one of the man-
made things called a cart trail. Along the edges of it were
two deep-worn, endless canyons that man calls wheel
ruts, and into the first of these fell four of her brood. Five
managed to scramble across, but the other rut was
deeper and wider, and there the five were also engulfed.

Oh, this was terrible! The little ones were all too
weak to climb out. The ruts seemed to go on forever in
both directions, and the mother did not know how to
help her babies. She and they were in despair, and as
she ran about calling and urging them to put forth all
their strength, there came up suddenly the very thing
she most feared—the deadliest enemy of ducks—a great,
tall man.

Mother Green-wing flung herself at his feet and
flopped on the grass. Not begging for mercy! Oh, no! She
was only trying to trick the man into thinking she was
wounded so that he would follow her, and she could lead
him away.

But this man knew the trick, and he would not follow.
Instead, he looked about and found the nine little bright-
eyed downlings deep in the ruts, vainly trying to hide.

He stooped and gently gathered them all into his hat.
Poor little things, how they did peep! Poor little mother,
how she did cry in bitterness for her brood! Now she
knew that they all were to be destroyed before her very
eyes, and she beat her breast on the ground before the
terrible giant in agony of sorrow.

The heartless monster went to the edge of the pond, no
doubt for a drink to wash the ducklings down his throat.
He bent down, and a moment later the ducklings were
spattering free over the water. The mother flew out on the
glassy surface. She called, and they all came scurrying to

her. She did not know that this man was really her friend; she never knew that he was the deliverer whose mere presence had driven the fox away and saved them in their direst strait. His race has persecuted hers too long, and she went on fearing him to the end.

She tried to lead her brood far away from him by taking them right across the open pond. This was a mistake, for it exposed them to real enemies. That great marsh hawk saw them and came swooping along, sure of getting one duckling in each claw.

"Run for the rushes!" called out Mother Green-wing; and run they all did, pattering over the surface as fast as their tired little legs could go.

"Run! Run!" cried the mother. But the hawk was close at hand now. In spite of all their running, he would be upon them in another second. They were too young to dive. There seemed no escape, when just as he pounced, the bright little mother gave a great splash with all her strength, and using both feet and wings, dashed water all over the hawk. He was astonished. He sprang back into the air to shake himself dry.

The mother urged the little ones to keep on. Keep on they did. But down came the hawk again, again to be repelled with a shower of spray. Three times did he pounce, three times did she drench him, till at last all the downlings were safe in the friendly rushes. The angry hawk made a lunge at the mother; but she could dive, and giving a good-bye splash, she easily disappeared.

Far in the rushes she came up, and called a gentle *quack, quack!* The nine tired little ones came to her, and safely they rested at last.

But that was not all. Just as they began to feast on the teeming insect life, there came a faint, faraway *peep*. Mother Green-wing called again her mothering *qu-a-a-a-a-c-c-k.* And through the sedge, demurely paddling like an old-timer, came the missing one that the hawk had carried off.

He had not been hurt by the claws. The valiant king-bird had overtaken the hawk over the pond. At the first blow of the kingbird's bill, the hawk had shrieked and dropped his prey, and the little duck fell unharmed into the water. He escaped into the rushes till his mother and brothers came; then he rejoined them, and they lived happily in the great pond till they all grew up and flew away on wings of their own.

59

 ## A Child of God

BY ELIZABETH WAGLER

For three hundred years before the events of this story, the Christian faith had been spreading steadily across the Mediterranean world—in spite of all attempts to suppress it. The Roman emperor Diocletian ruled between the years 284 and 305; and like his predecessors, he was suspicious of the Christians' quiet yet unyielding refusal to bow before the Roman gods. He became convinced that Christianity would mean the downfall of his government.

The emperor Diocletian slouched among the purple velvet cushions of the imperial throne, chewing impatiently on a fingernail. His eyes darted restlessly over the noisy crowd gathering in his Hall of Justice.

Today he would condemn another group of those traitorous Christians who refused to bow to his supreme power. He was determined to put an end to their efforts to undermine his leadership!

For a moment, the scowl left his face. A young man named Pancratius had stood before him yesterday, and he would be brought forward again.

Diocletian shifted his heavy body and drummed his

fingertips on the carved arm of his throne. The daring thought that had vexed him ever since he first saw the lad was still very much on his mind.

"Pancratius," he mused. His eyes softened. "He's the image of the son I never had." Diocletian frowned uneasily at the crowd through half-closed eyes. What would his senators and generals think if he made such an unprecedented offer? Would he dare to pardon one Christian in the face of his harsh persecution of others?

Resolutely he gripped the arms of the throne. Of course he dared! After all, he was the emperor. Who would dare to challenge his judgment?

"But what if the boy refuses?" Diocletian hesitated at this disturbing thought. He brushed it quickly away. Such a promising young man would surely be willing to become the son of the emperor. He knew the Christians were incredibly stubborn in clinging to their beliefs, but surely Pancratius would recognize the great opportunity . . .

"Marcullus!" Diocletian bellowed suddenly.

"Yes, sir!" A brawny centurion left a nearby group of armed men and hurried to answer the summons. He bowed low, his sword almost scraping the tile floor, and then snapped to attention before his master.

"Where are the prisoners?" demanded Diocletian. "I am ready for the day's trials. Station your men; tell those gossiping senators to take their places; bring in the prisoners immediately!"

"Right, sir." Marcullus saluted smartly and turned to carry out the command.

In a few moments, the crowd in the judgment hall came to order. White-robed senators took their places on either side of the throne. Imperial soldiers stood guard in orderly lines around the perimeter of the hall. As a noisy rabble of common folk crowded into the rear, Marcullus returned to Diocletian's side.

"The prisoners will be here shortly," he reported.

"Not that one—the young man?" Diocletian put in hastily.

"No, he is not among them. I remembered your orders; the youth will be brought alone."

"How many today?" An evil light glittered in the emperor's eyes.

"About two hundred. We found them worshiping in a ruin outside the city. Like the other groups, they offered no resistance."

Diocletian shook his fist in fury. "Worshiping, you say? Ha! Plotting, I say. If we cannot rid Rome of these treacherous Christians, our empire will fall. They must be destroyed!" He pounded the arms of his throne and shouted again, his voice rising with each new threat. "Destroyed, I say. I will drive them from their holes! I will purge my empire of their blasphemy! I will so utterly crush—"

At this moment the side doors swung open and a large group of prisoners started into the hall. A storm of jeers greeted their appearance as the jailers herded them toward the throne with slashing whips. Several of the mob threw rocks or chunks of broken tile at the captives. Yet there were those among the spectators who felt a twinge of pity as they looked on the group. Signs of suffering and ill treatment were obvious.

The prisoners' clothing hung in tatters as a result of the cruel beatings they had endured. Many limped painfully, and the strong supported the weak as they made their way toward Diocletian. But in spite of the severity of their lot, they uttered not a sound. Rather, there seemed to radiate from them an air of tranquillity and acceptance, the light of an inner peace.

The emperor wasted little time on them. He addressed the white-haired man who appeared to be their leader.

250

"You there, old man, do you not bow before me?"

The old man, looking squarely at Diocletian, quietly replied, "I bow before no man, sir; only before my God, who is Lord of all."

"So you refuse to worship the gods of Rome?" Diocletian's eyes blazed.

"It is written, 'Thou shalt have no other gods before me,' " the old man answered softly; and the lips of the other Christians formed the same words.

"Then hear this"—the emperor's voice rose to a high shrill. "Tomorrow morning all of you will be taken to the seaport and there locked in the hold of a ship. The vessel will be set on fire and left to drift out with the tide. If any of you wish to escape this death, you have only to bow before me and our great Roman gods."

There was not a sound. An almost imperceptible shudder seemed to pass through the group. At last the old man raised his eyes and spoke once again to Diocletian.

"May the Father of our Lord Jesus be glorified. Our lives are His," he said.

"Then die, you fools! Guards, take them away!" shouted the frenzied Diocletian.

As they were led, stumbling, from the hall, one voice began singing softly, "O God, accept our offering now . . ."

Diocletian roared with anger. "Silence!" he shouted, covering his ears with both hands until the sound of the hymn died away.

The emperor leaned back in his throne, breathing heavily, making a visible effort to still his rage. Gradually his manner changed. The hard lines on his face softened slightly. "Now, the young man," he ordered. "Bring him in."

While he waited, the emperor turned and spoke softly to his trusted centurion. "Are you certain the boy saw the tortures of yesterday's prisoners?"

"Yes," Marcullus answered, "he saw everything."

"Good! That will help. I intend to make him an offer he will not resist. I abhor these Christians; but this lad would make an admirable Roman if he could forget his foolish religion."

A hush fell over the room as a single prisoner was escorted to the throne. He was a youth of only fourteen. Thick brown hair crowned his head. Intelligent eyes gazed steadily toward the judgment seat. His handsome features and upright bearing caused many in the mob to wonder that such a fine lad would identify with the despised Christians.

"If only fate could have favored me with such a son," the emperor mused inwardly.

"Pancratius," he addressed the boy almost gently.

"Sir?"

"You have seen what became of the other prisoners?"

"Yes, sir."

"Do you wish the same fate?"

Pancratius bowed his head; then drawing himself up, he spoke in a voice that all could hear. "My Lord and Saviour bore great suffering for my sake; I should count it a great honor to suffer as He did."

"Nonsense," snorted Diocletian, taken aback by the boy's reply. "What have you against the Roman gods?"

"They are only images. 'We ought not to think that the Godhead is like unto gold, or silver, or stone, graven by art and man's device,' " quoted Pancratius. "The Roman gods have no power, but the true God has power to save the soul even though the body perish."

The emperor controlled his temper with difficulty. "My boy," he urged, leaning forward slightly, "I will make you an offer. If you will give up your religion and sacrifice to the gods of Rome—I will adopt you as my son!"

A shocked murmur rose from the watching crowd, and they pressed forward to hear the prisoner's answer.

"Well?"

Pancratius began to speak, his voice echoing through the hall. "When my Lord was tempted, He replied, 'Thou shalt worship the Lord thy God, and him only shalt thou serve.' I rejoice to share the same temptation that the Son of God endured, and I return to you His answer. I would rather die as a child of God than live as your son."

Diocletian was struck dumb; then his features darkened and he leaped to his feet. "Fool!" he screamed. "Soldiers, lead him out into the Aurelian Way and remove his head!" Cursing and raging, Diocletian stormed from the judgment hall.

And so the condemned Pancratius was led to his death, rejoicing that he was soon to meet his Lord.

Over sixteen hundred years have passed since Pancratius died for his faith. The Roman Empire, which Diocletian sought to defend by his persecution of the early Christians, has long since crumbled in the dust of forgotten centuries. But the kingdom of Jesus Christ for which Pancratius died will stand forever.

60

Composition Theme

The Good Samaritan

And, behold, a certain lawyer stood up, and tempted Him, saying, "Master, what shall I do to inherit eternal life?"

Jesus said unto him, "What is written in the Law? How readest thou?"

And he answering said, "Thou shalt love the Lord thy God with all thy heart, and with all thy soul, and with all thy strength, and with all thy mind; and thy neighbour as thyself."

And Jesus said unto him, "Thou hast answered right: this do, and thou shalt live."

But the lawyer, willing to justify himself, said unto Jesus, "And who is my neighbour?"

And Jesus answering said, "A certain man went down from Jerusalem to Jericho, and fell among thieves, which stripped him of his raiment, and wounded him, and departed, leaving him half dead.

"And by chance there came down a certain priest that way: and when he saw him, he passed by on the other side.

"And likewise a Levite, when he was at the place, came and looked on him, and passed by on the other side.

"But a certain Samaritan, as he journeyed, came where he was: and when he saw him, he had compassion on him, and went to him, and bound up his wounds, pouring in oil and wine, and set him on his own beast, and brought him to an inn, and took care of him.

"And on the morrow when he departed, he took out two pence, and gave them to the host, and said unto him, 'Take care of him; and whatsoever thou spendest more, when I come again, I will repay thee.'

"Which now of these three, thinkest thou, was neighbour unto him that fell among the thieves?"

And the lawyer said, "He that shewed mercy on him."

Then said Jesus unto him, "Go, and do thou likewise."

LUKE 10:25–37, *ADAPTED*

ACKNOWLEDGMENTS

We hereby express our gratitude to the following publishers for the use of materials:

"To Market," "Lito Finds His Way," "The Oil or the Book," "The Other Half of the House," from *Seven-Minute Stories* by Alice Geer Kelsey. Copyright 1958, Abingdon Press. Used by permission.

"The Second Mile," adapted by Florence M. Taylor in *The Storyteller in Religious Education*, by Jeanette Perkins Brown. Copyright 1951, The Pilgrim Press; renewal 1979. Valencia Perkins Burt.

"It's in Your Face," "Which Are You?," "Growing Smiles," from *Poems That Live Forever*, courtesy of Doubleday and Co.

"The Hunters," used by permission from W. G. Crisp, Vancouver, British Columbia.

"A Sweet Story," reprinted by permission of Hawthorn Properties (Elsevier-Dutton Publishing Co., Inc.). From the book *Cities of Wax*, by Julie Clossen Kenly. Copyright 1935, D Appleton-Century Co., Inc. 1963, Henry Clossen Kenly.

"James Dulin's Bargain," selected and adapted from *The Youth's Companion*, 1877.

"The Daisy," "The Crop of Acorns," selected from *Sanders New Fourth Reader*, 1855.

"The Better Way," selected from *The Standard 4th Reader*, 1865.

"It Is Common," selected from *The Book of Knowledge*, Vol. IX, The Grolier Society, Ltd., 1926.

"A Night on the Mississippi," selected from *The Jones Fourth Reader*, Ginn and Company, 1903.

"Our Daily Bread," "I Paused Last Eve," selected from *The Treasury of Religious Verse*, courtesy of Fleming H. Revell Co.

"The Rescue," selected from *Union Fourth Reader*, 1863.

"Hands That Shed Innocent Blood," rewritten from *Martyrs Mirror,* page 428.

"Susan's Temptation," from *The Third Reader* ("The First Tempation"), 1860.

"The Very School of Snow," selected from *The American Educational 5th Reader,* 1873.

"John Maynard," "The Plough," from *Story Hour Readings— 6th Year,* American Book Co., 1921.

"Perseverance," from *The Modern Grammar School Reader,* 1882.

"Mary's Bible," from *Mary Jones and Her Bible,* courtesy of American Bible Society.

"Rebellion in the Hive," from *Parables of Nature,* publisher unknown.

"The Brickfields of Bristol," from *Horseman of the King,* courtesy of Lutterworth Press, England.

"The Lost Boy," adapted from *Angell's 5th Reader,* 1853.

"The Basketmaker of Cavan," from *The Gen for 1849,* by Kearney. Rewritten by Dennis Good.

"Cyrus McCormick Invents the Reaper," from *How the Reaping Hook Became a Machine,* published by Milton Bradley Co.

"Sleep Sweet," courtesy of G. P. Putnam's Sons.

"The Mother Teal and the Overland Route," from *Lives of the Hunted,* courtesy of Schocken Books, Inc.

"Language Without *Love,*" from *Great Is the Company,* by Violet Wood. Copyright 1955, Friendship Press. Used by permission.